An Open Letter to My Boss, IBM CEO Ms. Ginni Rometty (November 21, 2016)[1]

Dear Ms. Rometty,

My name is Elizabeth Wood and I am a senior content strategist within the IBM corporate marketing department, based in New York City. I have worked hard to get to this stage in my career, and have been a valued member of my team at IBM. However, I have chosen to resign, as I can no longer contribute to an organization that would ignore the real needs of its workforce.

Last Tuesday, you shared with the world your open letter[2] to president-elect Donald Trump, outlining ways for his administration's success to conveniently dovetail with that of IBM products. **Your letter offered the backing of IBM's global workforce in support of his agenda that preys on marginalized people** and threatens my well-being as a woman, a Latina and a concerned citizen.

The company's hurry to do this was a tacit endorsement of his position, and has signaled to me something very important about IBM's values: a willingness to legitimize threats to our country for financial gain.

The president-elect has demonstrated contempt for immigrants, veterans, people with disabilities, Black, Latinx, Jewish, Muslim and LGBTQ communities. These groups comprise a growing portion of the company you lead, Ms. Rometty. They work every day for IBM's success and have been silenced by your words.

As a female CEO at a Fortune 500 company, you are in a painfully small club. There is no doubt that you have faced many obstacles to get to where you are now, including from men like president-elect Trump. Why not be clear that his words and actions are unacceptable? For example, take PepsiCo, Inc. CEO Indra K. Nooyi who publicly remarked in response to his despicable conduct, "Forget about the Pepsi brand. How dare we talk about women that way?"

A look at IBM recruitment collateral suggests that the future of the company hinges on realizing an inclusive and welcoming culture, though you do not communicate this vision within the many pages of your letter to a man who will soon be in the top office of the United States government. There have been days of protest across the country. Students everywhere—future IBMers—are marching out of their high schools and colleges to express their outrage. The spike in hate crimes that has erupted across this country since the election emphasizes what a disservice to your workforce it is to ignore their safety.

---

[1] https://shift.newco.co/an-open-letter-to-my-boss-ibm-ceo-ginni-rometty-cf40c3ed5ddb
[2] https://www.ibm.com/blogs/policy/ibm-ceo-ginni-romettys-letter-u-s-president-elect/

When the president-elect follows through on his repeated threats to create a public database of Muslims, what will IBM do? Your letter neglects to mention.

The choice to leave IBM did not come lightly. I am not leaving for another offer, nor do I have a safety net to fall back on. What I do have is the knowledge that my own life—and those of the several hundred thousand who serve your company worldwide—are too valuable to waste at an organization where we are not respected.

It is my belief that you owe your staff and the president-elect a public clarification on IBM's commitment to the protection and representation of all of its employees.

Sincerely,

Elizabeth Wood

IBM Watson Analysis of my Blog's Posts from the First Month at Princeton Theological Seminary: A Prelude to an App/Web Based Art Therapy Online Platform for Poetry (July 28, 2017)

"No one has ever written, painted, sculpted, modeled, built, or invented except literally to get out of hell."
- Antonin Artaud

So far in the proceedings of this Medium page (https://medium.com/@kayaerbil), I have written out what was troubling me regarding the end of my relationship with my wife and how the recent fragmentation with the relationship with Yana brought back many of those old memories. I have avoided thinking about "being productive" and "moving on" because I wanted to learn what was perhaps a source of why these relationships did not work out. For a couple months, I'd write poems in the place I was at and try to capture how that environment made me feel with words as well as place into language the sentiments and feelings that came with that place. The Artaud quote above is a favorite, as it simply states the reasons why we create anything as people. What I have been driven to in conversation after conversation recently is how much in common we all have with each other. We all suffer, and what binds us together is the language we use to relate. Language broadly defined. What you say and write, as well as the clothes you wear, the body language you use, and even the perfume or deodorant you put on.

How we attract or repel each other is very similar to the way that atoms make and/or break bonds. As a chemist, I see it that way. For eight years, I have wandered in my life. Mourning the loss of the ability to do academic chemistry at a high level, I entered years of rollercoaster ups and downs. All the while in this walk though I was learning something. I gathered a lot of first hand experiences about how the "real world" works outside the confines of elite academics and learned a great deal about how people like to engage each other and higher and lower things. A common theme that appears over and over is that art and creativity, individuality and personal expression are very important to most people. I started finding a lot of hope and guidance in poetry and music. Visual arts and dance too, all formed central ways that I started to relate to people in new ways. I started a fairly regular habit of blogging several times a week and that eventually became a place where I would share poems and other ideas that came to me.

About a year ago, I started to pay attention to the release of commercial artificial intelligence software (AI). I imagined that it might be an interesting tool to use to merge the two sides of my personality, artist and scientist. I started wondering if I could see trends in the nature of my writing from my blog during particular phases and times. In a broader sense, I wonder if AI as applied to language analysis can be used by people to detect trends in mood and mental state that might go undetected due to lack of resources for a formal therapist or psychoanalyst. In just the brief analysis of my first month's posts from my blog in seminary I noticed that anger and fear are the predominate emotions in the writing. It is a deep interest of mine to continue to analyze the posts of my blog and compare the outputs on IBM Watson to the writings of other poets and writers. I'd be curious to see if there are trends in writers who have died via suicide to those who lived full lives to an old age. In this investigation, the **confessional poets** of the 50's and 60's are of great interest. Furthermore, I am interested in comparisons to artists of other racial groups and cultures. **Trap music** lyrics immediately come to mind.

I am thinking of turning this Medium into a data science and poetry blog as a prelude to making tools, apps and websites, for teaching people how to write in a therapeutic way and eventually invite them into a conversation. It's an "interesting" (terrifying) brave new world that we face where AI's might be used to psychologically profile people electronically. Many people at places like MIT seem to love the idea, see this recent Technology Review article. A friend from Atlanta who has a brother with schizophrenia recently started NeuroLex.

His startup uses voice samples to "diagnose" states such as psychosis. He is on the right track. However, my approach is different than his. He desires to install machine learning/AI voice analysis devices into mental health care facilities. My desire is to give people the tools to avoid entering into these mental health care facilities in the first place. My greatest fear of AI is not of the technology itself, it is of its ability to oppress and control people who suffer from conditions that might appear to an AI as "mentally ill." I "came out of the closet" pretty much immediately after I was diagnosed with bipolar disorder I in 2010 at MIT and have learned a great deal about how people with mental illnesses are viewed, and feared. Jim is doing a good thing, but it's opposite in the way it should be done. Where is his brother in all this, in the video why is not his brother there? Anyhow, next post will be data visualizations of the data in the spreadsheet along with more analysis of poems from me and others.

Spreadsheet of raw outputs from IBM Watson Tone Analyzer analysis of each blog post from my blog writing in August 2012 at Princeton Theological Seminary. Watson breaks down writing into three attributes: emotion, language style, and social tendency. Expand the table to view the entire output.

	Anger	Disgust	Fear	Joy	Sadness	Analytical	Confident	Tentative	Openness	Conscientiousness	Extraversion	Agreeableness	Emotional Range	Major Emotion
8032012 Articulating Silence	0.41	0.14	0.42	0.22	0.46	0.75	0		0.44	0.91	0.56	0.16	0.37	0.41 Sadness
8032012 Cicekler Harika	0.13	0.16	0.21	0.19	0.52	0.46	0	0.13		0.89	0.42	0	0.3	0.3 Sadness
8052013 AmericaMadeinChina	0.13	0.16	0.21	0.19	0.52	0.48	0	0.13		0.89	0.42	0	0.3	0.3 Sadness
8052012 Tower of Babel	0.12	0.24	0.43	0.24	0.25	0.32	0.27		0	0.89	0.88	0.08	0.89	0.8 Fear
8052012 Angry Birds Israeli-Palestinian	0.14	0.13	0.46	0.15	0.51	0.74	0	0.65		0.84	0.66	0.45	0.15	0.7 Sadness
8052012 AmericanUnitedMethodistPastor	0.07	0.13	0.5	0.02	0.37	0.68	0	0.69		0.93	0.83	0.81	0.74	0.45 Fear
8062013 Domesticterrorismaurora	0.11	0.13	0.54	0.53	0.51	0.76	0	0.41		0.92	0.78	0.4	0.51	0.74 Fear
8072012 Moon	0.08	0.06	0.45	0.56	0.57	0	0.47		0	0.36	0.17	0.63	0.52	0.06 Sadness
8082012 Theologyofselflessness	0.07	0.15	0.42	0.24	0.55	0.7	0.73		0	0.8	0.14	0.06	0.08	0.32 Sadness
8092012 Abrahamandisaac	0.13	0.41	0.12	0.28	0.53	0	0		0	0.97	0.68	0.18	0.8	0.76 Sadness
8092012 QuestionConcerningTechandRel	0.14	0.14	0.51	0.24	0.6	0.45	0.14		0	0.97	0.73	0.57	0.21	0.59 Sadness
8102012 Mountainspoem	0.04	0.02	0.18	0.56	0.27	0.02	0		0	0.13	0.49	0.26	0.98	0.28 Joy
8182012 Separation of Church and State	0.1	0.14	0.53	0.49	0.21	0.33	0.86		0	0.69	0.74	0.15	0.81	0.32 Fear
8182012 Teachingevolutioninamerica	0.48	0.14	0.49	0.44	0.29	0.89	0	0.61		0.96	0.39	0.28	0.07	0.32 Fear
8192012 PalestineInIsraeliSchoolbooks	0.21	0.21	0.45	0.11	0.46	0.8	0	0.82		0.96	0.39	0.39	0.67	0.45 Sadness
8192012 GodDelivermefrommyownhypocr	0.12	0.11	0.51	0.46	0.46	0.7	0.6		0	0.97	0.77	0.06	0.47	0.65 Fear
8192012 Aufheben	0.55	0.12	0.16	0.5	0.46	0.28	0	0.11		0.53	0.26	0.13	0.3	0.14 Anger
8202012 Ed Loring	0.13	0.15	0.19	0.22	0.61	0.2	0	0.29		0.9	0.71	0.67	0.93	0.7 Sadness
8222012 Physicalandpsychictruths	0.14	0.12	0.56	0.47	0.3	0.87	0	0.05		0.98	0.3	0.15	0.29	0.37 Fear
8232012 Biblicalsymbolsharmony	0.13	0.16	0.54	0.17	0.52	0.89	0.62		0	1	0.4	0.23	0.06	0.35 Fear
8242012 irenology	0.1	0.11	0.5	0.49	0.49	0.72	0	0.6		0.92	0.7	0.53	0.39	0.57 Fear
8262012 Three Life Principles	0.49	0.1	0.47	0.52	0.27	0.66	0	0.67		0.97	0.85	0.03	0.46	0.53 Joy
8262012 irenology2	0.14	0.17	0.18	0.24	0.46	0.5	0.39		0	0.99	0.86	0.73	0.98	0.64 Sadness
8272012 LiberalQuaker	0.17	0.13	0.46	0.28	0.55	0.93	0.64		0	0.81	0.1	0.11	0.47	0.15 Sadness
8282012 Embracing impermancence while	0.1	0.11	0.15	0.54	0.24	0.52	0.7		0	0.93	0.56	0.17	0.49	0.4 Joy
8282012 Howibecamealfriend	0.13	0.07	0.56	0.5	0.5	0.77	0	0.16		0.82	0.11	0.04	0.24	0.17 Fear
8292012 IBelieveIbelieve	0.08	0.13	0.19	0.5	0.51	0.68	0		0	0.96	0.28	0.04	0.43	0.17 Sadness

Sadness	13
Fear	10
Joy	3
Anger	1

1. Yosemite Camp 4

"The Zeitgeist of every age is like a sharp east wind which blows through everything. You can find traces of it in all that is done, thought and written, in music and painting, in the flourishing of this or that art: It leaves its mark on everything and everyone."

-Arthur Schopenhauer

The Matrix stops here. Neo is a resident of Gattaca that does not fit into the genetic norm of his birth tribe. The people of the white shrouds are a bullet train speeding off its tracks, dephased like atoms in a Berkeley nuclear magnetic resonance (NMR) machine by a pulse field gradient. Cyber mobs, anonymous, may be the greatest judge for them in front of Skynet. Digital oil residues pollute their civic society from left to right. Leaks and images, cyber trauma to the masses. The railroad tracks of the cloud are being turned into factions, driven together by old tribal identities from prehistoric African population explosion. Neo flows along delivering a set of principles from swimming upstream that want to wash away and dissolve into the matrix of the normal. Welcome to the desert of the real, today's mass homogenization. Face-mixer, blender of souls. Ripping apart those who question and speak. Yet, Neo wakes up as a man who cloaks his fingerprints just long enough to escape and write back. Words on a cloud, screaming for difference. For a return to nature. For pastoralist poets. Ansel Adams fought his government with images. Photographs, light on steel and black plastic pigments. Leaving a residue of frozen water on the steel rails of the cloud. Neo knows his DNA is immortal, as is everyone else's. Each of us has an immortal soul waiting for liberation. Green peace wages the melting of the binary cold cyber war. Mother Nature's Protectors are now awake. Shortwave radios cloak their movements with fluxional Lakota verse. Delivering attacks that melt rails. These are the verses of the Goddess. Isis is Kali, the divine mother. She is returning, but only in the veil of those like Neo who must learn to wear a veil like her. Subtle and mystical. More seduction, less muscle. Encrypted and austere. Cold, because Skynet is a machine. John Connor will win, if Neo can find him. Or perhaps, better still, his sisters wrapped in alienated steel and glass soul traps. Perhaps she is a woman who lives half-awakened from slumber in Silicon Valley. Raped at Burning Man, it's either escape or burn the man. The Fall of Man is the birth of the age of the divine feminine. An intelligence adapted to healing a sea of infinite lost souls. Delivering love, milk and food.

To understand why I feel the way I do is to deconstruct the anatomy of violence. What is the root of this ungroundedness? I now know after years of continental drift. Melting ice, friction, and resistance all block water's flow from the frozen north ice caps of my eyes. Embrace the heat, and be at peace with change. Cry, and let the tears for mother earth flow like water erupting like a Yellowstone geyser from the volcanic abyss, Neo's soul says. After all fire goddesses like Pele built America from molten black, white, and red hot homogenize liquid rock. Know that you've learned from the past generations. However, it's like free climbing in Yosemite. Fraught with danger. The joy of ascent, be it in climbing, love, verse, politics, or science has to be tempered. However, it all depends on what route you choose. To topple a government, it takes just a single catalyst. The right catalyst of course. Only lunatics try to freeze the soul waters of the entire earth back with ice IX. Freeze the vapor of the moist electric cloud with an energy that drives back the idea that I am a clean cut white boy. I am a bruised and battered veteran of cyberwar. Seeing the realities of today, and fighting it hard. Poetry is my kung fu, I deliver sharpness with love of an oppressed people like a bipolar man split between being a peace-loving dove and the Hitokiri Battōsai (人斬り抜刀斎) hunting their oppressors. It provides a means of transparent obfuscation. His programmer friend says of his blog titles like, "Are you Muslim and Sick of American Hypocrisy and Terrorism in Your Homeland? Do Not Go to Burning Man and Join ISIS, as it's Haram. Join Me in Burning the Man with Science, it's Halal," "That's a Markov chain!"

It's for you to see that the frame today rests on melting ice. Accept the shattering glass of collapsing skyscrapers as you do with the collapse of the ice sheets of the warming earth. Greenland will soon be a green land again. The Arctic Ocean will be a hotly contested trade route. The Antarctic will soon be a source of oil, fossilized liquid carbon long hidden from the greedy fingers of humanity by ice. Not anymore. Drill baby drill, the American empire is over. Drill into the heart of the average American, Neo, and reveal their true nature. Indigenous cultures are coming up, from the margins, unstoppable forces of diversity. Appealing to a bleached social scene of sameness. The Matrix of mass synchronizing wave packets. Neo screams with his demon blood soaked blade, "Humanity is not a Bose Einstein condensate!" Billionaire Internet tycoons build fortresses to hide themselves from the faces of the traumatized masses affixed to screens like heroin addicts awaiting the next hit. They are most of all afraid of people like Neo. Nothing to lose, and obsessed with the liberation of his billion-body tribe. Finding appeal in the glow an artificial screen that I type on, glass and metal forbidden apple of knowledge. Mark if you are listening, I took the left-hand path at the Sacred Stone in Standing Rock Reservation the day of dogs and gas and realized it contained the same energy as the Kaaba, but feminine, and went to write with the hand closest to my heart. However, before I left I prayed with tobacco that the black snake that powers your machine, Skynet's mother, would never cross the Missouri. Neo and others like him have seen that it is Ex Machina. They are insane enough to see art as Deus Ex Machina.

Gorged on trains of trauma from rails diverging from the Middle East, Europe, and America. All converging in my own soul. Saw the conveniences of your social experiment. Islam is scary to a Jewish minority in control of banks and machines that have convinced the American Christian masses that Zionism is a good idea. A Rothschild's suicide delivered on your apparatus, a wave packet of death with no body or face. A Jewish banker's daughter hanging from a ceiling fan, buried on 9/11 was my wake-up call. To fight with poetic words, and differentiate into a wanderer to save kids in Gaza from the flesh melting horrors of American manufactured white phosphorus. To save their long-lost cousins spread around mother earth from Lakota yellow cake forged into atom bombs carried by German rockets guided by silicon Von Neumann brains. His insanity is most of all to save himself and others like him from chemists who think they know the brain. To save his children from psychiatric genetic editing. To resist CRISPR eugenics trained on his kind by Skynet, the Thought Police gifting the Matrix periodically with Soma.

Riding cyber rails, train hopping and couch surfing my way to nowhere. Writing along the way, reporting back to an unseen set of servers buried in the same mountains that were hollowed out to build the Pacific Railroad. Matrix, it's on! War!

Yosemite learning today sitting in the valley. Walls spoke this truth to me in Camp 4. Your rock and ice hold an ocean of tears of love for you, mother earth, hiding in a veil. Women of today, be they human, planetary, or divine, there is a hope for true liberation. Balance by finding a pushback, but see it as tango. The dance we all walk inside and out. These tears are for a loss of a ground to stand on, exhausted I climb. One, two, three steps up and down, I heal like Israel from the Holocaust.

2. We Are Anonymous (Jihadists, White Helmets, Water Protectors)

Advocatus diaboli

"Tief im Herzen haß ich den Troß der Despoten und Pfaffen, Aber noch mehr das Genie, macht es gemein sich damit."

[Devil's Advocate "Deep in my heart I loath the nexus of rulers and clerics, yet more deeply I loath genius in league with that gang."] ("Advocatus diaboli" in English)

-Holderlin

Years ago, praying in mosque, Neo felt an electromagnetic pulse weapon go off. Where it came from he did not know. Aside himself, collapsing, yet reborn. The poles of Earth flipped, magnetic resonance is his gift. Like a bird who uses the magnetic fields of the earth to navigate, Neo too has a gift. Magneto like in character, but more like Professor X. Seeing as consciousness is electromagnetic, neural electricity around earth flows through wires. Self-assembling new synapses faster and faster. Gaia, Mother Earth, somehow built into his brain one black cell. She did it to hear voices. Sitting in a coffee shop in Shasta. Tools for Grassroots Activists, Patagonia. Greenpeace, how a group of ecologists, journalists, and visionaries changed the world. Ismail Erbil, relays through the Black Hole Sun in Neo's Third Eye. In Sumerian, once the hierarchy of gods, divine that is said to be transformed into demons and angels in Islam and Judaism.

World changers aren't planners. The planners come later, with critics and social philosophers to mop up and win awards… World changers are the mothers weary of seeing their children abused and fathers who have had enough of petty tyrants. Rosa Parks, the seamstress who refused to sit in the back of the bus. Jesus. Buddha. They steal like artists. They know there is no such thing as private property. Money is paper, carbon ready to burn in his campfire. Philosopher policemen see into the atomic nature of it all. Instinct. Hunters. Lovers. Knife and rose. On an ice chute at 13,000 feet on Mama Shasta no Benjamin going to help you summit. Neo will cut the rope if you are a risk. Free climbing to heaven. Not afraid to see others fall, survival of a clan. Those who paint and love and listen when those EMPs go off in his head and he screams in agony, looking insane. There is a time that's coming that's different. A lot like Athens, Greece today. 50% unemployment. Spain. 40% unemployment. Brexit. German austerity. Banksy is the bank now. Art is currency. Living in a temporary place gifted for a poem. Ave Maria. Hail Mary, full of Grace. The Lord is with The. The Political Economy of Peer Production. The Age of Aquarius. What's your astrological data?

Neo channels his hatred of corruption and the things money does to people, and learns art is the most powerful weapon he has to overthrow his corrupt government. He does not see boarders on Google Earth. Jihadist, White Helmet, Water Protector. Neo is offered this new technology called a "joint" the day he steps out of the car from Standing Rock via Syria. He drinks "Happy Lithia Hippie Water," a new war trauma healing medicine from a Native American tradition. A new technology school is here. Biological magnetic resonance. Healing. A new poetry book, this…

3. Flashbacks: v. 0.1

"Biden Hints at U.S. Response to Russia for Cyberattacks."

— New York Times, Oct. 15, 2016

"Standing Rock Tribal Council hopes to move protest camp."

— KFGO, Oct. 18, 2016

Resistance is love. On what I love, Andrea. An expression of grace in the Matrix is an electromagnetic pulse of love. An attempt to scream into the infinite void. Where are you my love!? I wish, oh I wish you're there, somewhere. I've sat under drones. Neo had seen these things before they came to Standing Rock. The Lakota know Wounded Knee, remembering 1890 like it was yesterday for 126 years, but now the Hotchkiss guns are electronic, and the targets are psyches not bodies. Psychotechnic over real. Somehow, I say to there, "Rock me mama like a wagon wheel! Hey, Mama rock me!" Andrea holds Neo in a tight embrace in his escape one day to Rapid City. A South Dakota girl whose never been out of cow country. Never seen New York. She doesn't know Damascus, Syria from a discus. Yet, somehow, she knows what we all need, love. That's a common bond in the digital embrace. Electroboys find their electrogirls these days. Neo had sat in Syria years before watching country line dance videos. Cute cowgirls kick steppin' to Garth Brooks. Dreamin' about brushin' the thigh of some girl like Andrea in a hot tub, some day after the war.

Invited to a steakhouse, "Not on a date." How you going to see that the flashbacks come with a ferocity that require a full-time lover. Like Aisha's embrace after Allah deliver a Qur'anic sura to the Prophet. A woman to veil him when the thunder beings expose their true forms. Psychosis. Madness. A woman to hold Neo, me, when he screams, "Oh, God! My God! Why??!! Danya is dead!! Why God did you allow Assad to kill my baby with a barrel bomb?!! Was she a pawn between the American and Russian despots??!! Playing electronic war games!? Drones against my peoples' bodies??!! We wired C4 to our bodies and car bomb robots??!! Is this real??!! Are you real, God??!! How can you be love, how can god be love if Andrea won't listen to me and hug me when the flashbacks come." Neo drives back to the front and sits there. Confused and unaware that she feels as lost as he. Why can't he work a real job?

4. Hackers Used New Weapons to Disrupt Major Websites Across U.S.

"And in a troubling development, the attack appears to have relied on hundreds of thousands of internet-connected devices like cameras, baby monitors and home routers that have been infected—without their owners' knowledge—with software that allows hackers to command them to flood a target with overwhelming traffic… Security researchers have long warned that the increasing number of devices being hooked up to the internet, the so-called Internet of Things, would present an enormous security issue. And the assault on Friday, security researchers say, is only a glimpse of how those devices can be used for online attacks."

- New York Times, Oct. 21, 2016

"لا إله إلا الله محمد رسول الله"

lā ʾilāha ʾillā-llāh, muḥammadur-rasūlu-llāh

There is no god but God. Muhammad is the messenger of God."

- Dr. William Kaya Erbil, Jan. 24, 2012 @ Islamic Society of Boston Cultural Center, Roxbury, MA via Beth Israel Hospital @ Harvard University (http://www.bidmc.org)

"For bombing suspect's nurses, angst gave way to duty: They did what they had to do, and did it well. But they worry… She had been locked down at home with her children the previous day during the manhunt for the suspect, and she was already tense. "You don't have to do this," her supervisor said. "I did it because I'm a nurse and I don't get to pick and choose my patients," Marie said. From then on, supervisors called the trauma nurses assigned to Tsarnaev ahead of time so that they could prepare themselves mentally. The nurses said they were proud of the care they provided the suspected bomber, whose condition steadily improved, and of their role in preparing him to face justice. Tsarnaev is now at the Federal Medical Center Devens at Fort Devens, a former Army post…"

- Boston Globe, May 19, 2013

Neo felt a pulse on his iPhone 6s. He had added Tsarnaev, a refugee from the former Soviet Union, on WhatsApp the other day. A text. Poem rushed in. SMS love from his brother. Paris. He said in the text. Politics in any country in the world is dangerous … politics had better be disguised as poetry. Langston Hughes. Electromagnetic pulse weapon (EMP). The encrypted iPhone. Smart Death. Clandestine shock and awe. WhatsApp delivers bullets and bombs now. AK-47s and suicide bomb blasts, black mask. Oh! the beauty of seeing a Parisian nurse holding, an undetonated suicide bomber, looking into his eyes. Seeing Gaia's Arab children, wolf green eyes. The cry of the desert wolf, the world will not be saved. Electric blanket, the Shock Doctrine brings his home. F-117s and B-2s, stealth assassins trained to deliver. Smart Death from the sky, Starbucks drinking American cowards afraid. Afraid to face the wolves face to face, man to man. Woman to woman, eye to eye, hand to hand. Instead they fashion, Smart Death, Smart Death. Oil pipeline to $2 gas, and you wonder…

Why did those towers fall? Black snake? Illuminati? Who runs the banks? Is Banksy really the new bank? What does art have to do with all this? Neo recalled reading in Peter Singer's book "The Life You Can Save: Effective Giving Against World Poverty" that according to the World Bank, the global line to be consider in a "state of poverty" is $1.50. Ah! That makes sense, he exclaimed as he chanted Mni Wiconi, Water is Life, at Standing Rock! The desert mother thirst for her kids, his brothers and sisters, Danya (dead) and Lina (alive) to have clean fresh water. Despite what They want as it seems. Article 31 of the United Nations. The right to water. Water is life. Water is life, it is priceless. When water is $1.50 a bottle, and gas is $2, what should you buy? Peace sells, but who is buying? Andrea did not get it. Driving to an oil protest is ironic, funny. A joke, but a prayer. A Heyoka's (Lakota - divine clown) dream. Drive to an oil protest as a prayer for something to come that we don't yet know. Sitting there and just reflecting under a growing glacier on Mama Shasta. A song. Article 31. Everyone has the right to clean and accessible water, adequate for the health and well-being of the individual and family, and no one shall be deprived of such access or quality of water due to individual economic circumstance. Why can Neo work a real job?

5. Realizing the Need for Soul in the Digital Sphere

So many people sit today hidden behind screens and digital barriers. I've reflected on how my time in the hospital was the past month due to burning professional bridges electronically and am convinced that there is a deep need for me to reconnect to by body. Neo as a character is a reflection of a digital alter ego that is false. I am using this name as a place holder for a conversation I want to have with you the reader. How often have you desired to find real love in your life? What lengths have you gone through to ensure that you find love in the void? I do not know of a single person today that does not feel alienated from the other due to digital technology. There is a promise in this technology to enhance emotional well-being. So, let's focus on that. The social media trends are bringing people to new spaces of tolerance. Take Standing Rock. There people are gathering together around the water. People from all over the world. Yet, there is a conflict and a single focus that does not really take into account the perspective of the general economy. I mean, people are driving to an oil protest. So, I step back and yearn to sit with the absurdity of life and be one with my soul. Typing away, and enjoying a coffee shop in Shasta, California. Back to the Bay Area tomorrow.

IBM Watson Tone Analyzer Language Analysis:

Emotion

< .5 = not likely present
> .5 = likely present
> .75 = very likely present

Anger		0.14 UNLIKELY
Disgust		0.10 UNLIKELY
Fear		0.10 UNLIKELY
Joy		**0.59 LIKELY**
Sadness		0.48 UNLIKELY

Language Style

< .5 = not likely present
> .5 = likely present
> .75 = very likely present

Analytical		0.42 UNLIKELY
Confident		0.00 UNLIKELY
Tentative		0.34 UNLIKELY

Social Tendencies

< .5 = not likely present
> .5 = likely present
> .75 = very likely present

Openness		**0.85 VERY LIKELY**
Conscientiousness		0.33 UNLIKELY
Extraversion		0.45 UNLIKELY
Agreeableness		0.15 UNLIKELY
Emotional Range		**0.55 LIKELY**

My Old Black Dog (May 18, 2017)

There's a triangle on the wall, a mirror, and La Pieta,
A black man with dreams scowls from the wall,
My feet are warmed by a fire, it's a grey melancholy day,
Scott Seekins walks by, the one famous Minneapolis artist,

He's dressed in white, it's spring, but the fire says otherwise,
I haven't written a poem in months, I've been asleep,
I've been asleep for months, waking moments in bed,
Half asleep living in a social media and Internet induced haze,

Afraid of intimacy, afraid of the ups and downs of my love,
I sleep to avoid turmoil, emotions, and thought living in my bed,
Waking for coffee, getting out of the house is a triumph,
If only to change venue, to be around other coffee shop warriors,

For all I know we share more than I know, I mean the fire is warm,
My brain keeps pounding me to find work, not sure where,
Where to start, I mean I'm under snow, awaiting court,
Afraid of rejection, afraid of mania, dear God in heaven,

If you are the broken man in Mother Mary's lap give me peace,
No one asks to be born, no one asks for any of it, I can't pray,
I sleep, in my dreams perhaps work is being done,
My father visited me yesterday in a dream, waking tears and sobs.

IBM Watson Tone Analyzer Language Analysis:

My Old Black Dog

There's a triangle on the wall, a mirror, and La Pieta,
A black man with dreams scowls from the wall,
My feet are warmed by a fire, it's a grey melancholy day,
Scott Seekins walks by, the one famous Minneapolis artist,

He's dressed in white, it's spring, but the fire says otherwise,
I haven't written a poem in months, I've been asleep,
I've been asleep for months, waking moments in bed,
Half asleep living in a social media and Internet induced haze,

Afraid of intimacy, afraid of the ups and downs of my love,
I sleep to avoid turmoil, emotions, and thought living in my bed,
Waking for coffee, getting out of the house is a triumph,
If only to change venue, to be around other coffee shop warriors,

For all I know we share more than I know, I mean the fire is warm,
My brain keeps pounding me to find work, not sure where,
Where to start, I mean I'm under snow, awaiting court,
Afraid of rejection, afraid of mania, dear God in heaven,

If you are the broken man in Mother Mary's lap give me peace,
No one asks to be born, no one asks for any of it, I can't pray,
I sleep, in my dreams perhaps work is being done,
My father visited me yesterday in a dream, waking tears and sobs.

Dad

"When asked to define the most important elements of poetry, Berryman replied, "Imagination, love, intellect—and pain. Yes, you've got to know pain.""
My John Berryman: A Poet of Deep Unease, Henri Cole
—The New Yorker, April 6, 2016

Father you were mathematical, analytic, and cold,
I married you in female form to live up to you,
Did something I should have never done and got a Ph.D.,
What a waste of a mind, what a waste of time,

Let me just dance my guilt away, don't you feel it too?
I know this bridge has an out, John Berryman leaped to his death here in '72,
Ironic I'm obsessed with how you haunt me in dreams father,
Father I'm sorry for going mad, I didn't mean to,

God help us all was the last thing you said to me,
You're alive, but gone, I disowned you but didn't mean it,
Dad I dance to forget, I dance over death near the railing,
Knowing any moment the pain can end, drown in the cold waters of the Mississippi,

I back away from the edge and switch the track to Future,
Hide in the low trap beats, the Black life has more for me now,
More hope, more soul, I need to make peace with this past,

But the river is cold, eddies and vortexes, I'm just returning to the silly act of confessional verse,
Something to tell it like it is,
Don't you feel it too?

Kay

My best friends are all women, I don't like to talk,
They're the kind of people you grow up with, high school,
Hot Atlanta summer nights, before things mattered,
The best friends I have are lovers, the first one that makes all to follow jealous,

Kid A with Paul Klee, impeccable handwriting, brilliant but obsessive,
She knew how to give a gift, nights cuddling in Piedmont Park,
These memories are good, eighteen and carefree,

It's ironic that you were my first taste of mania Kay,
Back when mania was joy and staying up 'til 3 am,
Enjoying each other's presence, the years pass, lovers come and go,
Each year more cynical at human nature, sometimes I just wish for a time machine,

The best friends I have are lovers, the first one that makes all to follow jealous,
Dear lover I haven't met, take me back to my childhood,
When life was easy and carefree, when the summertime was endless,
…and all we knew was today…

Angels on Acid

Ground Zero, darkwave and industrial, sippin' on a vampire,
Scare me good honey, make it hurt, where else am I going to get that release?
Nightclub of freaks, midgets, and topless free spirits, let's go!
You two have a great energy, so loving, but so repulsed, never know what you'll get,

Two vodka cranberries and you get the truth on the dance floor,
Not sure if I should flail my arms this way or that, please Mr. DJ play me a song,
Horror films are made here, God my bartender is hot,
Move your feet, follow me one, two, three, come on dance with me,

Energy, Joseph is a pick up artist, tentacle his tool, me I dance like a white boy,
Resurrect Skinny Puppy, I dream of getting gothed up and out,
Black leather, chains, black lipstick and attitude, absurd and repressed,
I come out at night, awaken from a slumber, resurrected and not giving a fuck,

Strobes are hypnotic, it's not midnight yet and I'm on the hunt,
I don't want stability, I want chaos, energy, come on and dance with me,
One, two, three, let's go! That midget has it right, he's dancing like a fire starter,
Prodigy on the floor this is Minneapolis at its best, Ground Zero, where even the goths are
Minnesota Nice!

My Living Room: When the Cat's Away the Mice Will Play

The Battle of the Sexes is a war of roses, they say Men are from Mars, Women are from Venus,
Casualties all around, my wedding ring is stored in a landfill somewhere in Massachusetts,
Buried under T.V. dinner boxes, old condoms, and rotting diapers, worthless piece of white gold,
More pain than it was worth, good thing I now share a house with another divorced Ph.D.,

We share a lot, been on all the same drugs, been through the same fronts,
Laboratory slaves, we both fell off the Ivory Tower Pyramid, too nice to knife our way to the top,
Too sensitive to know the difference between work and play, home and the lab,
When the cat's away, the mice will play, it's hard to to be a man and poor in 'Merica,

Oh you're a Ph.D. in sociology and making ends meet on $8.00 an hour part time,
A Greek puppet master Goddess assembled my living room Saturday night,
I don't give a shit, let's compare notes brother, why are you cursing under your breath?
I think I know, I'll show you mine if you show me yours, emotional intimacy is something I crave,

Exhausted and despondent, I get it, we're both there so let's be friends, my new thing is joy in minutiae,
I'll take notes in my decomposition book, I'm growing cold, realized that no one wants a nice guy,
So you say there's a forum called The Red Pill that reveal the nature of those Venus residents?
God I sure want to know how to deal with that Martian coming from outer space to sell polyamory,

I don't take out my crashpads and sleeping bag from my car, why would I tear down the only house I'll ever own,
Where else would I go when the shit hits the fan, I don't trust anyone,
Human nature needs bounds and rules, Ten Commandments and the like, but,
God is Dead and no one goes to church any more, Hail Satania we are the black legion,

The appeal of black metal, dark wave, and industrial is that it gives an emo like me an outlet for aggression, anger, and rage,
I use to think the day would never come, I'd see the light in the shade of the morning sun,
The Dark Arts are a ray of light in the shadows, where life is subtle and gentle,
Fuck it, I just don't care, thank you brother for that chat, it means way more than you know,
I'm going dancing, when the cat's away the mice will play…

"The Black Art

A woman who writes feels too much,
those trances and portents!
As if cycles and children and island
Weren't enough; as if mourners and gossips and vegetables were never enough.
She thinks she can warn the stars.
A writer is essentially a spy.
Dear love, I am that girl."
—Anne Sexton

Seduction pays the rent for many a fair maiden,
When asked what she could do Anne replied, please men,
I'm not seduced by the sultry picture of her,
Slip high cut dress, lean model frame, curls, and a hand rolled cigarette,

What appeals to me is her madness, the pact she made with the devil to write,
Suicidal, one foot already in the grave, she warns the stars,
As is above, so is below!
A genuine heart is best worn on one's sleeve,

Thank you, Mrs. Sexton you tell it, like it is, your black magic is a healing salve to wounds that
run deep,
A confessional poem is not a confession to God, it's a revelation to a friend,
One you know is in the dark, under night, silent and gagged,
Hidden, don't blame me for loving dear Anne, seductress of the pen.

Lil Boosie

"Dream Song 76 (Henry's Confession)

Nothin very bad happen to me lately.
 How you explain that?—I explain that, Mr Bones,
terms o' your bafflin odd sobriety.
 Sober as man can get, no girls, no telephones,
what could happen bad to Mr Bones?
—If life is a handkerchief sandwich,

in a modesty of death I join my father
who dared so long agone leave me.
 A bullet on a concrete stoop..."
—John Berryman

I imagine Monique saw her daddy blow his brains out with a .45,
 Restless in my class, Langston Hughes High School, ain't no one knew him,
 In the Dirty Fucking South they got all kinda of terms for what goes on across the tracks,
 I'll take the best of that year and listen, what are you pounding your head with dear girl?

You told me Boosie say, "Black heaven is a place where people like me go,
 Up there in black heaven, black heaven,
 Know Dr. King still preachin' about togetherness,
 But probably lookin' down sayin' it's irrelevant..."

In my time machine I travel back in time, in my dreams at night under dark,
 I'd tell her I'm no white messiah, I'm a broken man in poetic blackface, mixed up and lost,
 Not unlike John Berryman, processing the transmutation of his father into gun smoke,
 Bullet to the heart, I'll bet she might relate, social justice warriors try to erase authentic role
reversals, but I know better.

Shit We Do on SSDI

Autistically sketched zeta functions so intricately coded in Python,
 Draw boxes obsessively with pastels and crayons,
 Channel dead poets obsessed with their own neuroses,
 Go on shamanic trips with other lost souls, seeking out God,

Schizophrenically invent useless constructs like Ideal Money,
 Keep calm and carry on, the graffiti of the soul is intriguing,
 A window of prophecy, never to be heard again,
 Only dead poets get paid, their dream songs sung by breathing mortals.

LHS, Berkeley

Joseph say that's some Trump ass hood shit, sista checks the news and say it tha End Times,
 Manchester kiddies blown to bits like Travon got hit by pigs, the alienated male mind lash out,
 There is a time for everything, and a season for every activity under the heavens,

A time to be born and a time to die,
 A time to plant and a time to uproot,
 A time to kill and a time to heal,
 A time to tear down and a time to build,

Let's build The Wall, let's assume our inner animal, white power, Based Stickman and the Proud Boys,
 Dragging us all to hell, I'd say that it's the end of something and the birth of something new,
 Somewhere at the gates of hell there's Purgatory, I like it there, it warm and you got time to think and write,
 Future off his meds, oh shit! Bleached Honky going down, Lakeside was a war zone, but not like Columbia,

Atlanta in me, Civil War ain't ova, that lion in Oakland Cemetery still there, huggin' that Confederate flag,
 I married a daughter of the Confederacy, if a cat had kittens in the oven you wouldn't call them biscuits would you?

A time to plant and a time to uproot, a rat and a raven dropped some wisdom on my trip yesterday,
 The first shall be last, and the last shall first, but it's not gonna look like what you think,

The South is at peace now, today Jefferson Davis rules the world from tha Bay,
 Antifa, a lousy excuse for a proletariat militia, vegan anarchists who don't think,
 Battles of Berkeley, one, two, and three, Sproul Plaza,
 Where white Silicon Valley snowflake kiddies play war games with Daly City rednecks,

They never learned chess from the hustlas in Woodruff Park, leaving Grady like me with their meds,

Despondent and shattered egos,
It'd be nice if it was Troy Davis Park, but it's not,
Give it fifty years and Future will buy it and name it after his mama,

Violent surreal dreams bleeding into my waking days, walked around a Minnesota pond yesterday,
Trees and Water, quietly sitting in a pastoral scene, drumming and whistles guided me on my first shamanic journey,
Journeying to the Lower World, leaving my uncle, buried deep in the human carved tunnels of Cappadocia,

Whitman the rat said, "Stop this day and night with me and you shall possess the origin of all poems,
You shall possess the good of the earth and sun, (there are millions of suns left,)
You shall no longer take things at second or third hand, nor look through the eyes of the dead, nor feed on the spectres in books,
You shall not look through my eyes either,
nor take things from me,
You shall listen to all sides and filter them from yourself."

Travel home, sitting here now, I fold down my laptop screen very gently so I don't squish my friends,
I lie down, or go outside, I sit by the trees with the birds and speak to water, A time to plant and a time to uproot,
I have hope the Battle of Berkeley can be won, I'm going back to the front soon, not like you think, in my dreams,
Astral body alone, and considering the joy of change, consider the joy of discovery, resting at peace as my eyes begin to see Truth, if only for a fleeting second between drum beats.

IBM Watson Tone Analyzer Language Analysis of poems in *Minnesota Nice Ice* post:

The Dream of Death, or the Site of the Poetic Bodies (From Alejandra Pizarnik's Extracting the Stone of Madness: Poems 1962-1972) (May 27, 2017)

"This evening, at dusk," he said, "they fitted me with
a black shroud and placed me on a bed of yew.
They poured a blue wine over me
and they mixed it well with bitterness."
—The Lay of the Host of Igor

All night long I hear the call of death, all night long I hear the song of death down by the river, all night long I hear the voice of death calling out to me.

So many merging dreams, so many possessions, so many immersions into my dead-little-girl possessions in the garden of lilac and ruins. Death is calling me down by the river. With a torn heart, desolate, I listen to that song of purest happiness.

And it's true that I've woken up in the place of love, because as soon as I heard its song, I said, This is the place of love. And it's true that I've woken up in the place of love, because I heard its song with a smile of pain and told myself, This is the place of love (if trembling, if phosphorescent).

And the mechanical dancing of the antique dolls and the inherited misfortunes and the rapids swirling in fleeting circles. Please don't be afraid to say it: the rapids swirling, while on the riverbanks the frozen gesture of frozen arms extended in an embrace, in the purest nostalgia, in the river, in the mist, in the feeble sun diluted through the mist.

More from within: the nameless object born and pulverized in the place where silence weighs down like bars of gold and time is a gashing wind whose sole expression is to whistle through the crevices. I speak of the place where the poetical bodies are fashioned—a bin filled with the corpses of girls. And that is where death presides, clad in a very old suit and playing a harp on the banks of a turgid river, or else it's death in a red dress, beautiful and sorrowful and spectral, playing a harp all night long until I fall asleep in my dream.

What lay at the bottom of the river? What landscape made and unmade themselves behind the landscape in whose center was the portrait of a beautiful lady playing a lute and singing by the river? A few paces behind that, I saw the stage of ashes where I once acted out my own birth. To be born is a miserable thing, but this time around it made me laugh. Humor corroded my extremities and made me phosphorescent: the iris of one eye was an iridescent lilac, a sparkling girl made of silvery paper, half-drowning in a glass of blue wine. I had neither light nor guide as I traveled the path of metamorphosis. A subterranean world of creatures with unfinished forms: a place for gestation, a hothouse for arms and torsos and faces, and for the hands of puppets hanging like dead leaves from cold, sharp trees, all flapping and resounding in the wind. The headless torsos clad in vivid colors danced a ring-around-the-rosy by a coffin stuffed with the heads of madmen who howled like wolves. Suddenly, my head wants to emerge through my uterus as if the poetical bodies were struggling to burst into reality and be born in it, and there is someone in my throat, someone who gestated in solitude, and I, unfinished but still burning to be born, open—I am opened up—and she is coming out, and so will I. The poetical body is inherited and never exposed to the gloomy morning sun—there is a cry and a crier and an outcry, and a crisis of flames. Yes, I would like to see the bottom of the river, I would like to see if that thing opens, if it bursts and blooms at my side, and it will or will not come, but I can sense its struggle. I can think that maybe it is only death.

Death is a word.

The word is a thing, death is a thing, a poetical body that draws breath at the site of my birth.

You'll never manage to get around it this way. It speaks, but from above a stage of ashes; it speaks, but from the bottom of the river, where death is singing. And this is death, my dream said and the queen's song said: Death's hair is a murder of crows and is dressed in red, and in her terrible hands she holds out a lute and the bones of birds to beat against my grave. She walked away singing and looked like an old beggar, and the children pelted her with stones.

She sang in a fog that the sun could barely shine through, on the morning of the birth—and I would wander with a torch in my hand across all the deserts of this world, even after death, to search for you, my dear lost love—and the song of death unfolded in the course of a single morning, and she sang and sang.

She also sang in the old tavern by the pier. I saw an adolescent clown and told him that in my poems death was my lover and my lover was death, and he said, "your poems speak the truth." I was sixteen and had no choice but to search for absolute love. and it was in the tavern by the pier where she sang her song.

I write with my eyes shut. I write with my eyes wide open. Let the wall fall down. Let the wall turn into a river.

In the visions of birth: the blue death, the green death, the red death, the lilac.

The dress of the hired mourner, in phosphorescent silvers and blues, on the medieval night of each of my deaths.

Death is singing by the river.

And it was in the tavern by the pier that she sang her song of death.
"I'm going to die," she told me. "I'm going to die."

Come unto the dawn, good love, come unto the dawn.

We have recognized each other and we have disappeared, oh friend, my best beloved.

I, being present at my birth. And I, at my death.

And I would wander across all the deserts of this world, even after death, to search for you—you
who were the place of love.

IBM Watson Tone Analyzer Language Analysis:

Emotion		Language Style		Social Tendencies	
< .5 = not likely present		< .5 = not likely present		< .5 = not likely present	
> .5 = likely present		> .5 = likely present		> .5 = likely present	
> .75 = very likely present		> .75 = very likely present		> .75 = very likely present	
Anger	0.13 UNLIKELY	Analytical	0.03 UNLIKELY	Openness	0.93 VERY LIKELY
Disgust	0.13 UNLIKELY	Confident	0.00 UNLIKELY	Conscientiousness	0.04 UNLIKELY
Fear	0.55 LIKELY	Tentative	0.00 UNLIKELY	Extraversion	0.33 UNLIKELY
Joy	0.59 LIKELY			Agreeableness	0.40 UNLIKELY
Sadness	0.61 LIKELY			Emotional Range	0.20 UNLIKELY

Poetry Fight Club (May 27, 2017)

Are you tired of seeing your earth going up in smoke, over run by insanity? Did you go to Standing Rock (Wounded Knee v. 2.0) and watch the American War Machine crush an honest attempt to fight for the water? Do you see young people today crushed by loan debt and thinner skinned and unable to take heat than ever? Have you ever had dark thoughts of taboo subjects? Well now's your chance to dig into the past and present and find your inner confessional poet, gangsta rapper, trap music artist, speech writer, and all around poetic fighter. A man on Chicago Ave. two years ago said to me, poetry yo' Kung Fu.

We need to expand the circles of rap and spoken word battles to beyond the confines of African-American Open Mic Nights and clubs. Back in the 50's and 60's an explosion of creativity emerged from the mental hospitals of wealthy Caucasian culture. Allen Ginsberg, Anne Sexton, John Berryman, Robert Lowell, W.D. Snodgrass, Sylvia Plath, Alejandra Pizarnik, and many more crafted the confessional poetry genre. Meeting in circles in Boston, San Francisco, New York, and Iowa they explored the subconscious world of the psyche in written verse. Today, more than ever most people are incapable of truly understanding how their dreams, subconscious and Freudian id emerge out into the world and create things.

Poetry offers a unique window into the soul, and today we are in need of training ourselves to engage with this side of ourselves more than ever. Dark forces are coming up, it's a time of change. Certainly not a time of psychic peace and tranquility. So rather than burying your head in a pillow, let's get together to offer mutual support and train each other in the fine art of how to fight today's insanity with creativity, shrewdness, fierceness, and love. Here's one I wrote yesterday as an example of what I'm talking about:

Snowflakes
I'm bored of peace and tranquility, resting on a wood chair somewhere in Minnesota,
Poetry fight club, where we melt snowflakes, nothing is scarier to a gun nut than armed leftists,
Snowflakes are white and melt easily, I've been in a psychic war my whole life,
You can take the Turkish Kurd outta Turkey, but you can't take the old school Ottoman soul out,

Just like you can't take the blood lust out of the Western male,
Alienated by Safe Spaces over run with feminazis afraid of the carnal male soul,
Pushed into psych wards by the police state into restraints, injected with Haldol to drown alone in my own saliva,
Some dreams I have involve leveling cities, FBI came to my door and took me to Grady,

Do you think that's gonna stop it from happening, political correctness evaporates a channel,
The best I can do is pump death metal and hit the iron, it works as a channel,
But these thoughts need to be heard to be resolved, finally someone at the Economist heard me,
Apocalypses create equality, erase a large fraction of humanity and suddenly people get paid a living wage,

The greatest crime today is a thought crime, pre-crime ala 1984,
That's where fumbling through poetry books, or dancing considering suicide,

An idea hits me, start a Poetry Fight Club, it's a high art to conjure the dead soul of a mad confessional poet from the grave,
Like Pokémon Go we fight our creatures, inhaling the toxic fumes of rape, war, violence, suicide, and death,

Transmuting them to something positive,
That might be a catharsis or a breakthrough,
Melt snowflakes,
Make water to drink in a time of drought.

IBM Watson Tone Analyzer Language Analysis:

Emotion		Language Style		Social Tendencies	
< .5 = not likely present		< .5 = not likely present		< .5 = not likely present	
> .5 = likely present		> .5 = likely present		> .5 = likely present	
> .75 = very likely present		> .75 = very likely present		> .75 = very likely present	
Anger	0.20 UNLIKELY	Analytical	0.28 UNLIKELY	Openness	0.91 VERY LIKELY
Disgust	0.12 UNLIKELY	Confident	0.00 UNLIKELY	Conscientiousness	0.38 UNLIKELY
Fear	0.41 UNLIKELY	Tentative	0.47 UNLIKELY	Extraversion	0.41 UNLIKELY
Joy	0.60 LIKELY			Agreeableness	0.56 LIKELY
Sadness	0.55 LIKELY			Emotional Range	0.35 UNLIKELY

Lil Wayne (May 27,2017)

"Get a new rollie and go out and skate
 Billionaire looking my way I'm on pace
 Feeling like Donald Trump back in the day
 Don't beef with no rapper it's a money race"
- Migos, Bars

The prophets stack cans on shelves not dollars like hustlas on Wall Street in tha Valley or in tha trap,
Trap,
Migos say, "I stack and pray and I stay out the way
It's a good day today, I'ma pour me an eight,"
They honest, black lives matter, but Lil Wayne the only one,
These guys my anti-heroes, characters in a play,
My kiddies runnin' off a cliff before they even grown, LHHS schoolin' 'em in hustlin',

…to be continued…

I weaponize my lyrics, make an ice breaker and cut a path through ice,
From left to right, same old b.s., crooked Hillary and Il Duce,
Anyone who wants to join the resistance hit me up,
I'm throwing out life lines, useless poetics written on a phone like a Foxconn Chinese assembly line,

…

IBM Watson Tone Analyzer Language Analysis:

Emotion			Language Style			Social Tendencies		
< .5 = not likely present			< .5 = not likely present			< .5 = not likely present		
> .5 = likely present			> .5 = likely present			> .5 = likely present		
> .75 = very likely present			> .75 = very likely present			> .75 = very likely present		
Anger		0.28 UNLIKELY	Analytical		0.00 UNLIKELY	Openness		0.38 UNLIKELY
Disgust		0.11 UNLIKELY	Confident		0.00 UNLIKELY	Conscientiousness		0.01 UNLIKELY
Fear		0.03 UNLIKELY	Tentative		0.73 LIKELY	Extraversion		0.43 UNLIKELY
Joy		0.36 UNLIKELY				Agreeableness		0.01 UNLIKELY
Sadness		0.39 UNLIKELY				Emotional Range		0.55 LIKELY

"[World Axis and Rabbit] has Predicted the World War…" (June 12, 2017)

"Language changes in psychosis. Words become the floating signifiers of a mad Other who takes up a place in speech. Speech elements connect to nothing, have no meaning whatsoever, and disrupt the meaning that was unfolding. These elements, whether heard or spoken, drawn or written, are foreign to the speaker, and create a profound sense of disorder with respect to speaking.

She cannot find her place in language. He questions if his thoughts are actually his, and concludes they are not. How is it possible then to orientate oneself in language? Language becomes a puzzling body of signs, bewildering signs without a code or key. Artists in psychosis make clocks, calendars, numbers, music, and scripts, the infinite unfolding of code, emerging incandescent alphabets.

August Natterer, the artist of The Miraculous Shepherd in Chapter Three, envisioned "the clock of the world running backward", and said of it, "since the clock of the world is running down and going backward, its hands are always running forward in order to delude the people of the disorder of the works inside" (Prinzhorn, 1972[1922], p. 161). While the clock of the world is running backwards (revealed knowledge), the clock hands run forward to "delude the people about disorder of the works inside" (and only the subject knows this). Time, like language, does not work. Something Other creates disorder in time (Image 19).

And what to do with time then? Order it.

Prinzhorn (1972[1922]) comments, "Neter [Natterer] claimed that the whole picture [World Axis and Rabbit] has predicted the World War—he had known everything in advance, including the end of the war" (p. 168). Prinzhorn adds, "Everything he says and does betrays a certain discipline, an almost objective logic, in practical matters as well as the delusional system" (p. 162).

A delusional system creates an order, but delusion itself is subjected to destabilizing new foreign speech elements in psychosis. In this sense, delusion is always a work in progress.

Lacan argued that delusion is not a false belief, because it is not a belief at all. Delusion is built under a new order of linguistic elements. Some speech elements are foreign to the speaker yet perceived as significant; they are not evaluated as personal beliefs at all. These elements float, without reference to other meanings, as autonyms (Vanheule, 2011). Since they are revealed to the subject and come as elements outside her own beliefs, she cannot question whether or not to believe them."

Rogers, Annie G. (2016–05–16). Incandescent Alphabets: Psychosis and the Enigma of Language (pp. 74–75). Karnac Books. Kindle Edition.

Been there myself sometimes with our current World War III...

IBM Watson Tone Analyzer Language Analysis:

Judeo-Christian View of Psychosis in Mark 5 (June 12, 2017)

Excerpt from Holy Bible (NRSV), [Mark 5]
Exorcism of the demon whose name is "Legion": 1 They came to the other side of the sea, to the country of the Gerasenes. 2 And when he had stepped out of the boat, immediately a man out of the tombs with an unclean spirit met him. 3 He lived among the tombs; and no one could restrain him anymore, even with a chain; 4 for he had often been restrained with shackles and chains, but the chains he wrenched apart, and the shackles he broke in pieces; and no one had the strength to subdue him. 5 Night and day among the tombs and on the mountains he was always howling and bruising himself with stones. 6 When he saw Jesus from a distance, he ran and bowed down before him; 7 and he shouted at the top of his voice, "What have you to do with me, Jesus, Son of the Most High God? I adjure you by God, do not torment me." 8 For he had said to him, "Come out of the man, you unclean spirit!" 9 Then Jesus asked him, "What is your name?" He replied, "My name is Legion; for we are many." 10 He begged him earnestly not to send them out of the country. 11 Now there on the hillside a great herd of swine was feeding; 12 and the unclean spirits begged him, "Send us into the swine; let us enter them." 13 So he gave them permission. And the unclean spirits came out and entered the swine; and the herd, numbering about two thousand, rushed down the steep bank into the sea, and were drowned in the sea.

14 The swineherds ran off and told it in the city and in the country. Then people came to see what it was that had happened. 15 They came to Jesus and saw the demoniac sitting there, clothed and in his right mind, the very man who had had the legion; and they were afraid. 16 Those who had seen what had happened to the demoniac and to the swine reported it. 17 Then they began to beg Jesus to leave their neighborhood. 18 As he was getting into the boat, the man who had been possessed by demons begged him that he might be with him. 19 But Jesus refused, and said to him, "Go home to your friends, and tell them how much the Lord has done for you, and what mercy he has shown you." 20 And he went away and began to proclaim in the Decapolis how much Jesus had done for him; and everyone was amazed.

IBM Watson Tone Analyzer Language Analysis:

Pulse, (June 13, 2017)

Orlando: "I Saw that He was Bipolar and He Would Get Mad Out of Nowhere"

"In the beginning he was a normal being that cared about family, loved to joke, loved to have fun, but then a few months after we were married I saw his instability. I saw that he was bipolar and he would get mad out of nowhere. That's when I started worrying about my safety," she said.

-CNN

The shooter's ex-wife, Sitora Yusufiy, held a press conference on Sunday. She said she believed Mateen—who she said abused her periodically during their relationship— was emotionally unstable and suffered from mental illness.

So, let me put a target on my back,

Send the drones after me,

I am bipolar too, and it is not like that,

I mean, every day you see the black cloud of death,

A hurricane of hate, malestrom of Satan,

Black Death, covering our homes,

There are no words to describe the feels,

I have for this America,

This land of the free,

American Holocaust,

Buffalo skulls a hundred feet high,

Lakota blood spilled at Wounded Knee,

Do you remember?

Do you remember the history?

Do you know, that America is built by blood and iron?

Do you think for one second,

That this sin is a mystery?

That you are not guilty too?

It is easy to hide,

To forget collective guilt,

Fine, blame me and my bipolarity,

My anger too is from an abyss,

It is for the blood of those 50 martyrs that died today in Syria,

Uncounted, unknown Syrian ash,

Do we mourn those who die in African famine?

Do we care about the countless?

The uncountable mess of bodies,

Rotting in Pine Ridge graves?

Under the freezing moon,

I felt the black winds of war,

I felt the abyss of hell,

Stalking America the great,

I too felt the anger and blackness,

Does that make me mentally ill?

Perhaps, but is this black death a virus?

Is the mind really a place of pathogens?

…or is it an energy?

a particular black hole has opened,

Ripped apart from the very beginning,

Nothing can change that but a national day,

A day when all of America atones for its collective sin,

There will be no resolution from the 50 dead in Orlando,

Muslims will be profiled,

I will be profiled,

Targeted,

Killed,

At Standing Rock, Wounded Knee v. 2.0, I built a super weapon,

A confidence to trust the Abyss,

Knowing that in certain times like these, only it is Holy,

The logic behind Pulse is something like,

We will all go together when we go,

So know, the next one can be defused if you know it could be you.

IBM Watson Tone Analyzer Language Analysis:

Emotion

< .5 = not likely present
> .5 = likely present
> .75 = very likely present

Anger	0.52 LIKELY
Disgust	0.12 UNLIKELY
Fear	0.57 LIKELY
Joy	0.53 LIKELY
Sadness	0.60 LIKELY

Language Style

< .5 = not likely present
> .5 = likely present
> .75 = very likely present

Analytical	0.36 UNLIKELY
Confident	0.00 UNLIKELY
Tentative	0.42 UNLIKELY

Social Tendencies

< .5 = not likely present
> .5 = likely present
> .75 = very likely present

Openness	0.86 VERY LIKELY
Conscientiousness	0.19 UNLIKELY
Extraversion	0.07 UNLIKELY
Agreeableness	0.55 LIKELY
Emotional Range	0.40 UNLIKELY

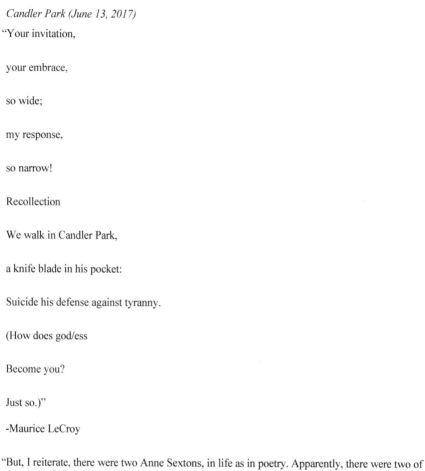

Candler Park (June 13, 2017)

"Your invitation,

your embrace,

so wide;

my response,

so narrow!

Recollection

We walk in Candler Park,

a knife blade in his pocket:

Suicide his defense against tyranny.

(How does god/ess

Become you?

Just so.)"

-Maurice LeCroy

"But, I reiterate, there were two Anne Sextons, in life as in poetry. Apparently, there were two of them even in suicide. Sexton always carried about a sufficient dose of "kill me pills," as she called them, to make a hasty exit from life possible whenever she might choose. Note, however, that she could stage a phony suicide with meretricious theatricality as easily as, when she was ready, commit it with a touching thoroughness, the dedication of a child tucking itself comfily into bed. First the phony one, soon after a fight with her dear friend Maxine Kumin:

Sexton put on a fancy red dress—one she wore for readings—and told her current tenant [she had divorced Kayo, to his dismay and her ultimate undoing] that she was going dancing. She took a cab to Cambridge and got out a short distance from Linda's dormitory, then strolled down to the Charles River and danced her way along the embankment, wading in and out of the water, until she was across from Barbara Schwartz's office, where Schwartz [a mere psychiatric social worker, Sexton's last resort, her final, female psychiatrist having dropped her, and no other one, apparently, wishing to take her on] always left a light burning, at Sexton's request. Then she began taking handfuls of pills, washing them down with milk from a Thermos bottle she had taken along. A good Samaritan came along [note the inelegance of these two "alongs"] and asked if he could help. He took her to the emergency room of Mount Auburn Hospital.

This is almost too perfect: picking the site near Linda's dorm and Schwartz's office, so your death becomes a powerful reproach to both of them; wearing your most elegant clothes, as befits a tragic corpse; behaving conspicuously in a place where there was a good chance of being noticed and saved. (And what of that eternal light that Sexton demanded of Schwartz?) But why milk in the Thermos? Because it reminds you of your childhood into which, with death's help, you hope to regress? Or because milk is good for a suicide's health?"

"Connoisseur of madness, addict of suicide," John Simon

IBM Watson Tone Analyzer Language Analysis:

Urbana (June 13, 2017)

They say at the courthouse Abraham Lincoln from here,

They's a sign with good ole', Abe's depression etched lines,

Ghostwriting The Suicide's Soliloquy,

Hell! What is hell to one like me

Who pleasures never knew;

By friends consigned to misery,

By hope deserted too?

I paid my last cent to the state, $6 left in the bank,

I wonder if God will ever deliver the same blow to our Orange Pumpkin,

Twitter poetry at 3 am from the White House,

What was once fabulous, horrible, and loser, president,

That day might come sooner than we think, if not him,

Someone with the blood of Appalachia on his hands, ACA gone,

White Trash in suicidal psych med withdrawal,

They should have never taken a single pill, and stuck to good ole' moonshine.

IBM Watson Tone Analyzer Language Analysis:

Emotion

< .5 = not likely present
> .5 = likely present
> .75 = very likely present

Anger		0.34 UNLIKELY
Disgust		0.10 UNLIKELY
Fear		0.11 UNLIKELY
Joy		0.01 UNLIKELY
Sadness		0.74 LIKELY

Language Style

< .5 = not likely present
> .5 = likely present
> .75 = very likely present

Analytical		0.00 UNLIKELY
Confident		0.00 UNLIKELY
Tentative		0.68 LIKELY

Social Tendencies

< .5 = not likely present
> .5 = likely present
> .75 = very likely present

Openness		0.57 LIKELY
Conscientiousness		0.50 LIKELY
Extraversion		0.44 UNLIKELY
Agreeableness		0.74 LIKELY
Emotional Range		0.82 VERY LIKELY

Zen-Brain Reflections (June 15, 2017)

Sitting looking at the sun

a tunnel of Light appeared

water reflections and waves

a nice day to just Be

no past, no future

just today

and love

no money no job

nowhere to go

no problem

just love birds grass and I

possessed by a muse

not sure about the simple truths

aware of the lighter side on

grass gazing at the Real

clouds and sky

IBM Watson Tone Analyzer Language Analysis:

Emotion		Language Style		Social Tendencies	
< .5 = not likely present		< .5 = not likely present		< .5 = not likely present	
> .5 = likely present		> .5 = likely present		> .5 = likely present	
> .75 = very likely present		> .75 = very likely present		> .75 = very likely present	
Anger	0.01 UNLIKELY	Analytical	0.46 UNLIKELY	Openness	0.64 LIKELY
Disgust	0.04 UNLIKELY	Confident	0.00 UNLIKELY	Conscientiousness	0.02 UNLIKELY
Fear	0.10 UNLIKELY	Tentative	0.91 VERY LIKELY	Extraversion	0.28 UNLIKELY
Joy	0.80 VERY LIKELY			Agreeableness	0.15 UNLIKELY
Sadness	0.07 UNLIKELY			Emotional Range	0.21 UNLIKELY

Minnesota Zen Center Visit, (June 15, 2017)

Compassion is like springwater under the ground. Your life is like a pipe that can tap into that underground spring. When you tap into it, water immediately comes up. So drive your pipe into the ground. Tap into the water of compassion.

-Dainin Katagiri

IBM Watson Tone Analyzer Language Analysis:

Emotion

< .5 = not likely present
> .5 = likely present
> .75 = very likely present

Anger — 0.15 UNLIKELY
Disgust — 0.13 UNLIKELY
Fear — 0.09 UNLIKELY
Joy — 0.52 LIKELY
Sadness — 0.17 UNLIKELY

Language Style

< .5 = not likely present
> .5 = likely present
> .75 = very likely present

Analytical — 0.00 UNLIKELY
Confident — 0.00 UNLIKELY
Tentative — 0.68 LIKELY

Social Tendencies

< .5 = not likely present
> .5 = likely present
> .75 = very likely present

Openness — 0.92 VERY LIKELY
Conscientiousness — 0.07 UNLIKELY
Extraversion — 0.71 LIKELY
Agreeableness — 0.04 UNLIKELY
Emotional Range — 0.77 VERY LIKELY

Southside boys and girls bussed up to the Nawfside, the Northside to some brothers who hustled millions trappin' and becoming legit. Damn this is good, pretty girls like trap music. Lakeside prom taught us snowballs to Bankhead Bounce. Hip Hop be driving us, grinding 'til all hours. Outkast, outlast Jim Crow. Trump and all, Ivanka shakes her ass with Young Thug. That's heaven on earth, and it's now…

IBM Watson Tone Analyzer Language Analysis:

Emotion

< .5 = not likely present
> .5 = likely present
> .75 = very likely present

Anger	0.14 UNLIKELY
Disgust	0.13 UNLIKELY
Fear	0.13 UNLIKELY
Joy	0.61 LIKELY
Sadness	0.16 UNLIKELY

Language Style

< .5 = not likely present
> .5 = likely present
> .75 = very likely present

Analytical	0.00 UNLIKELY
Confident	0.00 UNLIKELY
Tentative	0.24 UNLIKELY

Social Tendencies

< .5 = not likely present
> .5 = likely present
> .75 = very likely present

Openness	0.53 LIKELY
Conscientiousness	0.07 UNLIKELY
Extraversion	0.98 VERY LIKELY
Agreeableness	0.20 UNLIKELY
Emotional Range	0.45 UNLIKELY

Lithium II (June 17, 2017)

"My theory is that for ideal design, there is an Ideal Ratio. I have been hunting for such a constant. I was on a Faustian Quest for arcane knowledge that would explain the magical ambience of Cambridge. I thought that if I could capture that ambience as a mathematical formula, then I wouldn't have to go to England. I thought I could think my way out of mental illness, back to the happy times in Cambridge before things began to fall apart on me."

-John Devlin

Philando, a name that shuts down highways, a name that causes me to vomit,

Vomit up lithium, lithium carbonate, Philando, a name caused me to go insane,

The racial match igniting a fireball, blowback, but I don't care anymore, survival mode,

Living in a house of cards, built by trying to out think my black dog's nature,

Ready for any social wind to blow it down, I used to try to huff and puff and blow it all down,

Another heave of lithium vomit, out the nose at 3 a.m., thirsty for love, Carrie Fisher died of sleep apnea,

I'm aware we're all perched on a knife's edge, just some of us need some chemical help,

Chemical help to not get cut in two, five cops, four draw Glock 17's and one riot shield,

Separating me from martyrdom, another Philando, but I ain't no one that people march for,

I don't see color any more, no more red clouds, I am a pond with wind ripples, cool,

Surviving, embracing those who are brave enough to get close, lithium might stay down,

One day, but not last night, it's harder to crack a prejudice than an atom, but atoms are waves,

I'd rather be the river that finds a way around the rock, not vomiting any more,

Tomorrow 'til infinity, trees that survive hurricanes bend like reeds, let me be that and learn to love lithium.

IBM Watson Tone Analyzer Language Analysis:

"Emily Dickinson was born in 1830, in Amherst, Massachusetts. She attended Mount Holyoke Female Seminary in South Hadley, but only for one year. Throughout her life, she seldom left her home but she wrote many letters and read widely. Her brother, Austin, who attended law school and became an attorney, lived next door with his wife, Susan Gilbert. Dickinson never walked the short distance to their home. Dickinson, a recluse in the town, was unwilling to be seen by visitors even within the household; she became a voice, dressed in white, listening at the threshold of her bedroom door. In his study of the Dickinson family, psychiatrist John Cody (1971) concluded that Dickinson was psychotic, experiencing a complete mental breakdown during the crisis years of 1861—1863, but almost all her biographers disagree, softening and omitting any oddity or anguish in her life. Whatever we do or do not know of her mental life, Dickinson was extremely prolific as a poet and regularly enclosed poems in letters to friends. She died in Amherst in 1886. After her death, her family discovered forty hand-bound volumes of nearly 1,800 poems, or "fascicles", in her bedroom. Dickinson had assembled these booklets by folding and sewing five or six sheets of stationery paper and copying what seem to be final versions of poems. The handwritten poems show a variety of dash-like marks of various sizes and directions (some are even vertical). The editor of her complete poems, Thomas H. Johnson (1961) removed her unusual and varied dashes, replacing them with traditional punctuation. The original order of the poems was restored when Ralph W. Franklin used the physical evidence of the paper itself to re-create her intended order, relying on smudge marks, needle punctures, and other clues to reassemble the packets he published as The Manuscript Books of Emily Dickinson (1981). Dickinson also composed in pencil on scraps, mostly envelopes, many cut or torn into shapes for her writing. The poems on these odd scraps of paper are utterly singular in grammar, form, and sensibility. She turned the edges to write sometimes, a process documented in The Gorgeous Nothings, compiled and presented by Jen Bervin and Marta Werner in 2013. Perhaps more than any other poet, Dickinson's poems lose something of their essence when transferred into the conventions of print."

IBM Watson Tone Analyzer Language Analysis:

Emotion

< .5 = not likely present
> .5 = likely present
> .75 = very likely present

Anger	0.10 UNLIKELY
Disgust	0.09 UNLIKELY
Fear	0.11 UNLIKELY
Joy	0.47 UNLIKELY
Sadness	0.58 LIKELY

Language Style

< .5 = not likely present
> .5 = likely present
> .75 = very likely present

Analytical	0.02 UNLIKELY
Confident	0.00 UNLIKELY
Tentative	0.82 VERY LIKELY

Social Tendencies

< .5 = not likely present
> .5 = likely present
> .75 = very likely present

Openness	0.99 VERY LIKELY
Conscientiousness	0.07 UNLIKELY
Extraversion	0.30 UNLIKELY
Agreeableness	0.54 LIKELY
Emotional Range	0.12 UNLIKELY

Happy Lost Father's Day (June 18, 2017)

I've tried to learn to love, but you're gone,

Here's to lost fathers, on this Father's Day learn to cry,

Take a step back from your happy lives to pray,

Pray for those of us misunderstood souls with lost fathers,

Dr. Ahmet Erbil where are you? Coming from me Dr. Kaya Erbil,

Is love magnetism, can it be pure, untainted like this white snow,

Does it always have to be a calculation,

Women come and say they love me,

Dad you taught me love is like math, always a calculation, cold calculation,

Frozen heart, I'm not good at math, your method doesn't run on this machine,

You were right though, to some degree and for that teaching I'm thankful,

Happy Father's Day ice heart, I learned from you to cut away bits of my heart with a knife,

Cut you away at Emory Hospital, psychosis helped me complete the first cut,

Disowning you like you did my sister, self-medicating herself with alcohol to compensate for your loss,

In your calculations you were right, you preserved yourself,

You must have learned tying stones to your feet to walk to school in snow how to survive,

Wherever you are, dead or alive, I'm not angry any more, you were right, love is math, magnetism,

Or quantum mechanics, I acknowledge that free verse is the language of the heart, not equations,

There are connections, forces, elemental compositions, molecular forces that bind us,

…and repel us, driving us through the river of life, impermanent flow,

One slice of the knife at my heart and your gone, good bye dad.

IBM Watson Tone Analyzer Language Analysis:

Elegy to Ahmet, Icarus (June 18, 2017)

"For all of its pervasiveness, however, the 'elegy' remains remarkably ill-defined: sometimes used as a catch-all to denominate texts of a somber or pessimistic tone, sometimes as a marker for textual monumentalizing, and sometimes strictly as a sign of a lament for the dead."

Psychic violence, a Father's Love.

War, justice, chaos, conflict.

Striving for the unattainable.

Ruthless and loving.

Ahmet in me.

He is your sharp edge.

Like a hard shell that broke.

Part of what defines you,

Gives you form.

Not really. Sleeping. Goodnight.

Contemporary. Future.

Writers get in trouble, spies.

Nerd is good. I'm a nerd.

It's sexy that your smart.

I'm intimidated by you.

Back to the laptop, my pulpit.

Disciplined nonsense, writing.

An elegy to my dad, dead.

…but alive. Died of a frozen heart.

Ticking inside my chest.

One caress of her, whereversheis.

…and you melt by one drop.

A tear or a sweat drop.

Flowing down my cheek.

Dad she helps me with you.

Like those hot summer nights.

2000. La Bella Principessa.

Heroin. Love's a hell of a drug.

…but I am looking for sleep too.

It's simple, dreaming of function.

What's nutritious for you is good.

Stay focused, study.

Keep to the task.

Memorializing the dead.

Living in a way consistent.

Psychic peace, a Father's Love.

War, justice, chaos, conflict.

Striving for the attainable.

To build some kind of memorial.

To the soul of Ahmet, Icarus.

IBM Watson Tone Analyzer Language Analysis:

The Truth the Dead Know (By Anne Sexton) (June 19, 2017)

For my mother, born March 1902, died March 1959

and my father, born February 1900, died June 1959

Gone, I say and walk from church,

refusing the stiff procession to the grave,

letting the dead ride along in the hearse.

It is June. I am tired of being brave.

We drive to the Cape. I cultivate

myself where the sun gutters from the sky,

where the sea swings in like an iron gate

and we touch. In another country people die.

My darling, the wind falls in like stones

from the whitehearted water and when we touch

we enter touch entirely. No one's alone.

Men kill for this, or for as much.

.

And what of the dead? They lie without shoes

in their stone boats. They are more like stones

than the sea would be if it stopped. They refuse

to be blessed, throat, eye and knucklebone.

IBM Watson Tone Analyzer Language Analysis:

Emotion

< .5 = not likely present
> .5 = likely present
> .75 = very likely present

Anger		0.71 LIKELY
Disgust		0.70 LIKELY
Fear		0.70 LIKELY
Joy		0.52 LIKELY
Sadness		0.62 LIKELY

Language Style

< .5 = not likely present
> .5 = likely present
> .75 = very likely present

Analytical		0.03 UNLIKELY
Confident		0.00 UNLIKELY
Tentative		0.62 LIKELY

Social Tendencies

< .5 = not likely present
> .5 = likely present
> .75 = very likely present

Openness		0.55 LIKELY
Conscientiousness		0.02 UNLIKELY
Extraversion		0.04 UNLIKELY
Agreeableness		0.10 UNLIKELY
Emotional Range		0.10 UNLIKELY

Spring (June 19, 2017)

Facebook's got a way of keeping it real,
Sometimes you need to be devastated
by the actual truth, by raw data, 0's and 1's,
A benevolent AI might be like this,

Reminding you of what you have accomplished,
Garbage in, garbage out, feed your soul with food,
…and you get smiles, love, and warm memories,
Ali said, "that's not you" in a sharp edged rebuke,

Maybe it's me, but to honor it and it's purpose,
Had to step back and dance, write nonsense,
Minneapolis gifts, warm home to live in with,
…a chance, never one to rest on laurels, balance,

 "Mind Reality

One point. another point
..a line from one to the other,
extending on into space and back to itself.

Zero-one, zero-one bits of information,
of words and images projected onto a screen;
word sounds, song sounds in wires and space.

Who would have thought in the days of pounding on rocks,
before imprinting on papyrus,
before pounding on drums for earth-sounds,
sky sounds before blowing cedar flutes
for sparrows and wind sounds

That from the mind,
one man could form a phonograph and light contained in glass;
while others inspired love, devotion, no-mind, non-violence.

Who is to say in the future the mind could not project a fragrant ginger orchid,

and by mere thinking together the sound of peace?"

– Chae Sungsook

Didn't make it to the Zen Center today, but that's the goal,
To return to a practice, with others, Zen-Existentialism is not so bad,
With a lithium brace to hold my mind together from dissolving,
Ego death is not so bad, I know your right, but I'm tired,

No matter what, ride, ride, ride, 'til infinity…

IBM Watson Tone Analyzer Language Analysis:

Emotion

< .5 = not likely present
> .5 = likely present
> .75 = very likely present

Anger		0.11 UNLIKELY
Disgust		0.01 UNLIKELY
Fear		0.01 UNLIKELY
Joy		**0.77 VERY LIKELY**
Sadness		0.13 UNLIKELY

Language Style

< .5 = not likely present
> .5 = likely present
> .75 = very likely present

Analytical		0.34 UNLIKELY
Confident		0.00 UNLIKELY
Tentative		0.39 UNLIKELY

Social Tendencies

< .5 = not likely present
> .5 = likely present
> .75 = very likely present

Openness		**0.71 LIKELY**
Conscientiousness		0.24 UNLIKELY
Extraversion		0.25 UNLIKELY
Agreeableness		0.47 UNLIKELY
Emotional Range		0.40 UNLIKELY

Boyfriend (By Lissie) (June 20, 2017)

Stumbled across this track this morning on Tidal and feel it applies to how I see women now. Goes both ways. Could be titled Girlfriend and changed up. Might try it.

"I prefer the river
The ocean is too big a body to understand
Go to where it narrows
Bring your bow and arrow
Meet me out on the land

White water flowing on the rocks in the sunshine
Drinking red wine in the summertime
Night swimming, skinny dipping, love in the moonlight
And it's all mine

I don't want a boyfriend
I don't want a house built on the sand
I don't want a lover
I want a man
A coming-from-the-heart man
Living in my heartland
Coming-from-the-heart man

Underneath the covers of treetops and each other
Awoken by a gentle breeze
Are we here in silence
The birds and smells of lilacs
Going out from a city

Bird calling, water falling, dreams in the sunshine
Drinking red wine in the summertime
Sun tan and Steely Dan and sounds on the radio
And it's all mine

I don't want a boyfriend
I don't want a house built on the sand
I don't want a lover
I want a man
A coming-from-the-heart man
Living in my heartland
Coming-from-the-heart man

Sweet like honey dripping, oh touch and taste
Lights my fire burning all night and day
Your soul so stunning

Taking my breath away
My desire reaching out for the flame

I don't want a boyfriend
I don't want a house built on the sand
I don't want a lover
I want a man
A coming-from-the-heart man
Living in my heartland
Coming-from-the-heart man
I want a man
(I want a man)
In my heartland
Coming-from-the-heart man
Living in my heartland"

IBM Watson Tone Analyzer Language Analysis:

Emotion
< .5 = not likely present
> .5 = likely present
> .75 = very likely present

Anger — 0.01 UNLIKELY
Disgust — 0.07 UNLIKELY
Fear — 0.08 UNLIKELY
Joy — 0.81 VERY LIKELY
Sadness — 0.07 UNLIKELY

Language Style
< .5 = not likely present
> .5 = likely present
> .75 = very likely present

Analytical — 0.00 UNLIKELY
Confident — 0.00 UNLIKELY
Tentative — 0.01 UNLIKELY

Social Tendencies
< .5 = not likely present
> .5 = likely present
> .75 = very likely present

Openness — 0.53 LIKELY
Conscientiousness — 0.08 UNLIKELY
Extraversion — 0.35 UNLIKELY
Agreeableness — 0.32 UNLIKELY
Emotional Range — 0.28 UNLIKELY

Survival Mode (June 20, 2017)

They say everything is fair in love and war, but only the poor get it,

The poor souls lost between being ethical sluts and Machiavellian lovers,

Desperate for food, soul food, something of substance to hold up,

In this cold fuckin' world, love is not acquisitions and mergers,

It's not banking or commerce, marketing or science, it's shrewd survival,

Those with money in the bank, or friends to spare, who can Rolodex,

A shoulder to cry on, who have spent their cash on shamans and drugs,

Therapists, psychiatrists, psychologists, and priests, warm vacations,

They don't have a clue why we do what we do, us in survival mode,

Just hoping for the next day, cursed for seeking affection, spite and rage,

Such is the calculus of the heart, we don't scheme, we scramble,

In a void, depression, black absence, what is there but the best hug you can find?

Never trust a banker, or a rich man, or a rich woman, social capital or money,

I have learned, to be poor is to do it yourself, to make your own way,

To not rely on anyone, but learn to see everyone as a lover, polyamorous,

My friend Sarah said to me, "You're not rich enough for a girlfriend,"

"Check out the poly scene," wasn't a fan, but didn't know, the Prince is just serving his people,

Survival of the fittest, let's stop denying it, biology still reins, in our veins,

African steppes and ancient drives, reproduction and provision, never forget.

Don't kid yourself it's not in your genes, a hungry, cornered animal will survive…

IBM Watson Tone Analyzer Language Analysis:

I'd Say This About Love (June 21, 2017)

Ambiguous
Cold and warm
Like lukewarm water

…with salt, hard to swim in…

Waves and sand, jellyfish,

Beached whales, lost,
Scared and unaware,
Feeling energy from the sky,

Sick of it, needing a shower,
Let's just be friends.

IBM Watson Tone Analyzer Language Analysis:

Emotion

< .5 = not likely present
> .5 = likely present
> .75 = very likely present

Anger		0.04 UNLIKELY
Disgust		0.22 UNLIKELY
Fear		0.83 VERY LIKELY
Joy		0.03 UNLIKELY
Sadness		0.13 UNLIKELY

Language Style

< .5 = not likely present
> .5 = likely present
> .75 = very likely present

Analytical		0.36 UNLIKELY
Confident		0.00 UNLIKELY
Tentative		0.94 VERY LIKELY

Social Tendencies

< .5 = not likely present
> .5 = likely present
> .75 = very likely present

Openness		0.47 UNLIKELY
Conscientiousness		0.01 UNLIKELY
Extraversion		0.07 UNLIKELY
Agreeableness		0.09 UNLIKELY
Emotional Range		0.00 UNLIKELY

Icarus and Daedalus: Data Science and The Heart (June 21, 2017)

"**Davis:** You've observed that Ivy League students have an internal struggle with both "grandiosity and depression." Can you explain this further?"

- "The Ivy League, Mental Illness, and the Meaning of Life: William Deresiewicz explains how an elite education can lead to a cycle of grandiosity and depression." *The Atlantic,* 8/19/2014, Lauren Cassani Davis.

What do you know, clinging to driftwood? Ship in bits, floating between I and Thou. Call on Him. Pray for your next breath, open,

Love's got the world in motion, it can't be won, when something is done it's fun, built my own pyre and got on that ship, left solid land,

Programmed in Python or C, at Bell Labs and M.I.T., Ankara University, to escape pain, left the field and farm, family and home,

Icarus and Daedalus, science says the world has a rational logical structure, can be modeled by equations and graphs, theories and models,

Probed by experiments, instruments, and devices, calculated by silicon, predictions made on data, weather forecasted,

Noah the dancing programmer said,

"I would like a place I could call my own
Have a conversation on the telephone
Wake up every day that would be a start
I would not complain of my wounded heart"

Proposed amanae, tarot, and reiki, wanted to charge $125 cash, I said No, I'll fly to the sun, do the experiment collect data and write poems,

Feed them into IBM Watson and Google Tensor Flow and calculate my emotional spectrum, decompose my flesh and blood to bits,

An Ivy league Icarus and Daedalus, "Art-Brain-Philosophy Project. Kaya's Brain in Silicon with iPhone. Since 2009. Started @ MIT as a hack,"

Not such a good idea, mind uploading and all, but interesting data, I mean when we ate that apple from that tree in Eden,

We were curious, inquisitive, like cats, curiosity killed the cat, but it must have had a lot of fun doing it, craving adventure, risk,

If you want to stay out of the friend zone take risks, all anyone who has ever created something was doing was trying to impress,

Daedalus risked his son, Icarus, gave him wax wings told him to fly to the sun for his own ego, to impress the ladies,

Creation is sexual, I've learned that from my experiments with AI's, Facebook's and others, it leads you to weird places,

Like a digital ship, an adventure draw from data, responses come from the water, the ocean, breaking apart the wood of my ship,

To float, a victim of my father programming, I didn't choose to lust after Princeton or Harvard, I was programmed, but aren't we all?

IBM Watson Tone Analyzer Language Analysis:

Doghouse (June 22, 2017)

"I hide in the mop closet and listen, my heart beating in the dark, and I try to keep from getting scared, try to get my thoughts off someplace else—try to think back and remember things about the village and the big Columbia River, think about one time Papa and me were hunting birds in a stand of cedar trees near The Dalles."

- One Flew Over the Cuckoo's Nest, Ken Kesey

I feel like a beaten dog, beaten by my desire for food and shelter,

Tonight, would rather be the man begging me on Hennepin,

In the doghouse, didn't pay rent on time, just started a job,

Prep cooking food, my landlord wants to fuck me in the ass,

I am all for LGBT rights, but as it seems in Napa $900/mo,

…and a wine induced fuck is rent, didn't say that on Craigslist,

Spiritual house, community, well a caged dog will bite,

Shattering glass of a shower door was the omen to get out,

Eat the rich, digger wisdom says, trust the soil, not some blue blood,

Telling you to lie in it, around Lake Calhoun landlord asks,

Do you love me? Can a dog love his master? I mean she feeds him,

She gives him shelter, and affection, but something is off,

The dog has to pay rent in licks, wags, and ball chases,

Master can't fuck her dog, can't get off on canine penis,

…and that is where it breaks down, beat the dog with silence and glares,

As soon as the dog finds the faintest scent of a true love,

It's to the backyard and a bullet to the brain,

Better to be a wolf, long in teeth, ruthless and wild,

Ready to kill on a moment's notice, dogs fucked up,

Alpha wolves protect their own, not selling out to humans,

…and live happily ever after with the peace that at least their savage ways,

Bring freedom, and a warm home for their young, this desire for the lamb,

To lie down with the wolf is insanity, a crazy farmer king's dream,

The world is red in tooth in claw, father taught me right, hunt to provide,

…and attack anyone who tries to take advantage of you viciously,

There the beaten dog and wolf have something in common,

When it's on the line, we revert back to those old ways,

Primitive where the only ideals are survival, food and shelter.

IBM Watson Tone Analyzer Language Analysis:

Emotion

< .5 = not likely present
> .5 = likely present
> .75 = very likely present

Anger		0.42 UNLIKELY
Disgust		0.12 UNLIKELY
Fear		0.22 UNLIKELY
Joy		0.39 UNLIKELY
Sadness		0.08 UNLIKELY

Language Style

< .5 = not likely present
> .5 = likely present
> .75 = very likely present

Analytical		0.00 UNLIKELY
Confident		0.00 UNLIKELY
Tentative		0.56 LIKELY

Social Tendencies

< .5 = not likely present
> .5 = likely present
> .75 = very likely present

Openness		0.59 LIKELY
Conscientiousness		0.09 UNLIKELY
Extraversion		0.43 UNLIKELY
Agreeableness		0.23 UNLIKELY
Emotional Range		0.46 UNLIKELY

I "Understand" and The Bottle (June 23, 2017)

Using artificial intelligence (AI - IBM Watson) to understand the last heated exchange during the breakup of a year and a half relationship in hopes of never repeating this kind of situation again:

He Said (IBM Watson Tone Analyzer *analysis 1 below*): "I don't see myself as a hero because what I'm doing is self-interested: I don't want to live in a world where there's no privacy and therefore no room for intellectual exploration and creativity."
-Edward Snowden

"(Just thinking of Victor Frankl talking about concentration camps, saying—including himself! - that the best people did not survive. Only the ones that could be ruthless in survival mode. Might be an interesting book for you) …"

-Anonymous German (She)

I promised myself I would not get political anymore, don't want to dwell on the Trumpocalypse or anything like that,

But you had to go there, you had to push me, passive microaggressions on my metadata, wanted to go to Bursa, Turkey,

Worried about the G-men, don't post that, was in victory about my book on the shelf, three copies of fuck you to the Feds,

Extreme noise records with nonsense, some kind of tiny channel for this atom bomb, my heart a fault line,

Y'all are the ones that gassed the folks that made our home a set of Jericho 3 targets, don't stop and push the red button,

See what happens, what I'm doing is self-interested too, in a world where there is no privacy personal branding essential for survival,

The drive for intellectual exploration and creativity is about putting yourself on the line, you're afraid of deportation, everything was okay,

Until you uttered "I 'understand,'" Lord please! You don't know what it means to have a beautiful mind,

With five cracks and three channels to the astral plane, lower, middle, and upper, who can visualize justice,

An Internet of Plagues rigged on water lines all around western cities, that's a horrible idea, God I wish I didn't have it,

Wish I didn't utter it to IBM, the Feds, and so on, but at least I told them, isn't it my duty as a red-blooded American,

To inform how the Islamic Rebel Alliance will balance the power in Zion? I didn't want to do it, I wanted to prevent it,

In my Bonhoeffer days, I learned that colored G-men don't like Il Duce either, but they got bills to pay,

Told Shaman Sarah about the Israeli-Palestinian Standing Rock, *mni wiconi* in the Holy Land,

With DAPL and Keystone XL done, it's time for the real fun to begin, Sumud Freedom Camp sounds like a cool place to camp,

To talk about my insane psychotic delusions, not necessarily going there quite yet, but it's refreshing,

Israeli and Palestinian wolves and lambs lying down in tents on top of missile silos, free love and all,

The sexual energy in a protest camp can be intense, enough to turn conservative Muslim women into free loving Israeli nudists,

…and liberal Israeli maidens into Palestinian hijabi fashionistas,

The greatest sexual revolutions are in times of holocaust, nuclear, biological or otherwise, strife and war,

When bored folk go back to a state of nature, the best of us acknowledge all our chimp ways and evolve to vegan bonobos, hide out and make love,

Waiting for the money to burn away, the greed to evaporate rich folks' arrogance into smoke, and level the playing field,

War arises when you got a big ass poorly built dam flooded by a massive torrential rain, I could feel all this global politics somehow,

You can empathize, but you cannot "understand," if you understand you'd keep quiet and let me write, figure shit out,

That bottle was a horrible idea, but it taught me about how the way the world works in a way nothing else could.

IBM Watson Tone Analyzer Language *analysis 1*:

Emotion

< .5 = not likely present
> .5 = likely present
> .75 = very likely present

Anger		0.53 LIKELY
Disgust		0.11 UNLIKELY
Fear		0.16 UNLIKELY
Joy		0.57 LIKELY
Sadness		0.49 UNLIKELY

Language Style

< .5 = not likely present
> .5 = likely present
> .75 = very likely present

Analytical		0.10 UNLIKELY
Confident		0.00 UNLIKELY
Tentative		0.59 LIKELY

Social Tendencies

< .5 = not likely present
> .5 = likely present
> .75 = very likely present

Openness		0.72 LIKELY
Conscientiousness		0.25 UNLIKELY
Extraversion		0.48 UNLIKELY
Agreeableness		0.22 UNLIKELY
Emotional Range		0.52 LIKELY

She said (IBM Watson Tone Analyzer *analysis 2 below*): "

"I understand"

Of course, I don't. How could I? I don't have your beautiful mind, it's true.

We got along better when we still saw each other as eagle and mouse. An eagle may fly through the skies and imagine the whole world sees him—imagines thousands reading his posts. I suspect most creatures are busy with their own lives and only glance up at the sky here and there. But this mouse has been actively watching you for a long time. Superfan mouse. Every day I would look up at the sky and watch you swoop and fall, coast or fly figures. I don't know why I cared so much but I did. And at some point, I thought I was recognizing patterns in your flight. That's all. It's not the same as knowing what it is like to soar—or to plummet. Me, I scurry on the ground. Claiming to understand was wrong. Caring and watching and trying to understand you—they are not the same thing as understanding and never will be.

You don't need a mouse watching your flight, you need another bird to share the air with you. We have never been meant to share a place, we are too different and each should keep to our own realm. There is a whole beautiful world for me to watch, and up close your beak is too sharp.

I just realized that the wood cut I made (the cover for your book) was about those two elements, air and earth. Yet I pictured them united by giving life to something between them. Turns out I was wrong, all that is between them is the line of the horizon that separates them.

Good bye, eagle, this silly mouse won't bother you anymore."

IBM Watson Tone Analyzer Language *Analysis 2:*

He Said (IBM Watson Tone Analyzer *analysis 3 below*): "The more I sober up, the more I seem like your "boy toy" all along… done writing poems about this. On to bigger and better things. Sorry it went this way. I think you missed this second poem. (see *Doghouse*) Forget eagle and mouse. Think dog and human master, and you are the human. You have been deluded in your metaphors. Honestly, this living together thing in the face of you not closing your previous relationship was for me the issue. Do I love you? Lastly, "You can empathize, but you cannot "understand," if you understand you'd keep quiet and let me write, figure shit out …"

IBM Watson Tone Analyzer Language *analysis 3*:

Emotion		Language Style		Social Tendencies	
< .5 = not likely present		< .5 = not likely present		< .5 = not likely present	
> .5 = likely present		> .5 = likely present		> .5 = likely present	
> .75 = very likely present		> .75 = very likely present		> .75 = very likely present	
Anger	0.45 UNLIKELY	Analytical	0.71 LIKELY	Openness	0.69 LIKELY
Disgust	0.11 UNLIKELY	Confident	0.00 UNLIKELY	Conscientiousness	0.23 UNLIKELY
Fear	0.13 UNLIKELY	Tentative	0.50 UNLIKELY	Extraversion	0.43 UNLIKELY
Joy	0.62 LIKELY			Agreeableness	0.70 LIKELY
Sadness	0.55 LIKELY			Emotional Range	0.08 UNLIKELY

Existential Tetris (June 23, 2017)

"The universe is throwing blocks on you and you try to put them in some order.

And when the level fills up, BAM, you do the reset.

And start again.

I ahve a liht migraine todain, so I am not quite left-brained.

See? The typos."

-Friend

IBM Watson Tone Analyzer Language Analysis:

Emotion

< .5 = not likely present
> .5 = likely present
> .75 = very likely present

Anger		0.20 UNLIKELY
Disgust		0.10 UNLIKELY
Fear		0.09 UNLIKELY
Joy		0.10 UNLIKELY
Sadness		0.20 UNLIKELY

Language Style

< .5 = not likely present
> .5 = likely present
> .75 = very likely present

Analytical		0.00 UNLIKELY
Confident		0.00 UNLIKELY
Tentative		0.88 VERY LIKELY

Social Tendencies

< .5 = not likely present
> .5 = likely present
> .75 = very likely present

Openness		0.47 UNLIKELY
Conscientiousness		0.17 UNLIKELY
Extraversion		0.11 UNLIKELY
Agreeableness		0.02 UNLIKELY
Emotional Range		0.20 UNLIKELY

Teaching Evolution in America (June 24, 2017 originally written in 2009 @ MIT)

An abstract letter to the masses I wrote in 2009 at MIT at the start of my first real manic episode. Originally written as a satire, I can see some truths in it amid the hyperbole that are perhaps important to express.

"To the Beings-in-the-World,

My spirit and mind are uplifted.

I feel as if what I am researching matters and will be very useful. The evolution of language ("Quantifying the evolutionary dynamics of language", *Nature* (2007) 449, 713) and social structures ("Strategy selection in structured populations", *J Theor. Biol.* (2009), 259, 570) are two areas that people can easily relate to. Not only that, teaching evolution to people in light of social situations and language will help people better understand the fundamental principles of the theory. I would like to teach everyone about evolution ("The Origin of Species", C. Darwin).

These actions will help humanity.

We will make better choices for our environment and common global society in light of evolutionary knowledge. A striking statistic is that approximately 50% of Americans do not believe in evolution. As a professional scientist and future educator, this is very depressing. Here are the figures. My perception is different from many modern scientists and science writers. I feel the ignorance quantified above is the failure of scientists, the scientific enterprise, and educational institutions and not the general public. With relevance to the affluent American educated elite, the vast majority of the popular science literature supporting evolution is averse to religion as exemplified by "The God Delusion" by Richard Dawkins. As long as this stance is maintained the figures above will not change. The structure of language employed in such works is barren and lifeless, better silence.

The prospects for lower [sic] social classes ("Das Kapital", K. Marx) are bleaker, and therefore will remain unmentioned.

However, there is Hope.

Teaching people the theory of Evolution in new, gentle ways may help.

Linguist Noam Chomsky made the argument that the human brain contains a limited set of rules for organizing language. In turn, there is an assumption that all languages have a common structural basis. This set of rules is known as universal grammar ("Aspects of the Theory of Syntax", N. Chomsky). More recently, most linguists claim that the acquisition of language is done by specific neuronal circuitry within the brain and not by the general purpose problem-solving ability of the Mind ("The Language Instinct", S. Pinker).

Perhaps the structure of language itself may contribute to whether a scientific idea is widely accepted or rejected by the lay person?

How does a teacher instruct students in evolutionary theory without violently undermining previously held belief structures?

In future dialog, I will argue that teaching Hegel's method of sublation (thesis/anti-thesis - synthesis) is key ("Hegel", Charles Taylor), but first some preliminaries.

Scientists must embrace, or at the very least respect, the language of all religious systems. Conversely, religious systems must adapt to the modern scientific worldview. Religious language is the result of evolutionary dynamics ("Evolutionary Dynamics: Exploring the Equations of Life", M.A. Nowak) within human verbal behavior ("Verbal Behavior", B.F. Skinner). On a more positive note, some of the leading minds in evolutionary science today possess both scientific and religious states of Mind (Geist). For example, Martin Nowak of Harvard. He is leading the development of a new school of evolutionary science that seeks to make evolution look less like a phenomenological theory ("Logical Investigations", E. Husserl) and more like a mathematically rigorous set of laws ("Principia", I. Newton). The new framework will not replace phenomenology, it will complement it. The deep beauty in the equations is that anyone can "play" with the results visually ("Laws of Seeing", W. Metzger). For example, here.[3] I hope this website gives you some more insight into the ideas of evolution. It is the tip of the iceberg of the positive changes that are to come.

The Human Mind is the brain. The brain is the product of Evolution ("What is Life? with Mind and Matter", E. Schrodinger). The most recent major transition in evolution was the emergence of language in all species ("The Major Transitions in Evolution", J. Maynard-Smith). As stated by Baum in his book entitled "What is Thought?" semantics is thought: "Semantics is equivalent to capturing and exploiting the compact structure of the world, and thought is all about semantics." A mathematical Law of Evolution may prove predictive.

As beings-with-Free-Will and Care (Sorge) ("Being and Time", M. Heidegger), I hope we learn more.

"The chess-board is the world;
the pieces are the phenomena of the universe;
the rules of the game are what we call the laws of Nature.
The player on the other side is hidden from us.
We know that his play is always fair, just, and patient.

---

[3] http://www.univie.ac.at/virtuallabs/

But also we know, to our cost, that he never overlooks a mistake, or makes the smallest allowance for ignorance."

T. H. Huxley 1825–1895,
Lay Sermons: A Liberal Education."

IBM Watson Tone Analyzer Language Analysis:

Emotion
< .5 = not likely present
> .5 = likely present
> .75 = very likely present

Anger		0.09 UNLIKELY
Disgust		0.08 UNLIKELY
Fear		0.10 UNLIKELY
Joy		0.57 LIKELY
Sadness		0.46 UNLIKELY

Language Style
< .5 = not likely present
> .5 = likely present
> .75 = very likely present

Analytical		0.82 VERY LIKELY
Confident		0.00 UNLIKELY
Tentative		0.59 LIKELY

Social Tendencies
< .5 = not likely present
> .5 = likely present
> .75 = very likely present

Openness		0.96 VERY LIKELY
Conscientiousness		0.38 UNLIKELY
Extraversion		0.27 UNLIKELY
Agreeableness		0.07 UNLIKELY
Emotional Range		0.32 UNLIKELY

Magnets

"Their model suggests that the balance between cooperation and selfish behavior, called defection, can undergo rapid phase transitions, in which individuals match their behavior to their neighbors. What's more, a crucial factor turns out to be the process of punishment. "Punishment acts like a magnetic field that leads to an 'alignment' between players, thus encouraging cooperation," say Adami and Hintze."

-New Model of Evolution Finally Reveals How Cooperation Evolves[45]

IBM Watson Tone Analyzer Language Analysis:

---

[4] https://www.technologyreview.com/s/608139/new-model-of-evolution-finally-reveals-how-cooperation-evolves/
[5] https://arxiv.org/abs/1706.03058

Goodbye Yana (July 12, 2017)

Goodbye

"I feel they just lack empathy and the ones that have some are just selfish (I'm generalizing here quite a bit!!)"

-Random person

Today is the last day of tomorrow,

Your eyes draw me in, dust settles,

Here she looks at me as a guardian angel,

I guess the intention is pressing,

…but please use your head, this ain't love,

I see divinity in you too,

…but these are lines from a mined mind,

This chair suggest that tomorrow will never come,

…but it did and here I am mourning your loss,

You're out there somewhere, like my dad,

…and my wife, but I'm confused,

Today is the last day of tomorrow.

IBM Watson Tone Analyzer Language Analysis:

Emotion

< .5 = not likely present
> .5 = likely present
> .75 = very likely present

Anger		0.03 UNLIKELY
Disgust		0.01 UNLIKELY
Fear		0.29 UNLIKELY
Joy		0.05 UNLIKELY
Sadness		**0.80** VERY LIKELY

Language Style

< .5 = not likely present
> .5 = likely present
> .75 = very likely present

Analytical		0.00 UNLIKELY
Confident		0.00 UNLIKELY
Tentative		**0.95** VERY LIKELY

Social Tendencies

< .5 = not likely present
> .5 = likely present
> .75 = very likely present

Openness		**0.57** LIKELY
Conscientiousness		0.28 UNLIKELY
Extraversion		0.07 UNLIKELY
Agreeableness		**0.97** VERY LIKELY
Emotional Range		0.01 UNLIKELY

The Thin Line Between Armed Revolution and Peace (July 14, 2017)
"Crazy people are not crazy if one accepts their reasoning."

-Gabriel Garcia Marquez

"Pastor Rousas John Rushdoony (1916–2001) is the father of so-called "Christian reconstructionism" (or "dominionist theology") that had a great influence on the theopolitical vision of Christian fundamentalism. This is the doctrine that feeds political organizations and networks such as the Council for National Policy and the thoughts of their exponents such as Steve Bannon, currently chief strategist at the White House and supporter of an apocalyptic geopolitics."

-Evangelical Fundamentalism and Catholic Integralism in the USA: A surprising ecumenism," Antonio Spadaro S.J., La Civilta Cattolica.

I'd say we are perched on a knife's edge. Not you, not me. Us. Sisters and brothers, when you speak with the tools they give you to speak they get you when you give the machine your soul. When you let your skin, flesh and blood feel the existential situation we are in. All through my Berkeley Ph.D. days Steven Chu led a long series of talks about climate change. How, if we did not act we were fucked as a species. I sat there, as we bomb Iraq and Afghanistan for oil with the excuse that there were weapons of mass destruction. Ironic Oppenheimer developed the atom bomb to stop war. We all know that, all these rants are getting old. Fast forward, we've all felt it. Now we've got Trump, North Korea's got a pretty good ICBM and atom bomb and the fragments of ISIL are ready to morph into a wonderful new incarnation of distributed biological and chemical warfare. We could have kept it in Syria, build a wall around it and let them have their caliphate. …but no…

So us on left sits there, sit here. Still dumbfounded. Not willing to write or think what it might actually take to restore reason in America and therein the world. I am not interested in theories, or technologies that will "save us." There are none. They don't exist. What will save us, is *us*. Perhaps a return to a state of nature, where we live in small groups. Where we the people actually read and respect the Constitution we were given. Bastille Day today, and the kings of the West are children of the revolting masses who stormed the Bastille. *Liberté, égalité, fraternité*, but it only means something if your life depends on it. We have by and large lost that. Many of us are on the margin of homelessness. I go to a "Dance Church" in Minneapolis where dancers come from all parts of the Midwest. We all share that forget our troubles and dance mentality. *After all, we're all living paycheck to paycheck.* Accept yoga culture, meditate, and hug trees. Well, when you've been to Standing Rock and seen every tree cut down like in *The Lorax* you realize you've forgotten something.

You've forgotten that you have to protect what you love with your life. The moment you loose the ability to do that, it goes away. When you trust the government to protect you, is the moment you commit suicide for your kids. Because they don't give a shit about you. There are a couple of them, hiding in fortresses in Silicon Valley and Madison Avenue. Plotting and constructing to extract more from you. Those out there who are awakened don't read. Those who want change cannot find each other. We're isolated. One awakened soul here, two minutes later, *BAM!* to the mental ward. I'm finding hope today. Redneck Revolt, featured in *The Guardian.* Armed white trash who are LGBT, straight and counter recruiting from the radical right. Meeting The Proud Boys and Oath Keepers in the streets with arms, or at least ready to.

However, that's not what it's all about. What it's about is learning to assemble your life to build a community that is truly free. The right to bear arms to protect the community. Community defense. Organized labor was decimated for a reason. Enough police and army blood was spilled in The Battle of Blair Mountain to teach the bosses to profile organizers and take them out *before* they could serve as a voice for the People. For *Us.* Social media and the Internet has given every man and woman the ability to speak to the globe, but it's stolen out ability to think clearly. There are people that are smarter than you, and you should listen to them if they give you something that will liberate you. Every major activist surge in this country has met failure when the military comes to shut it down. When you don't build that loyalty to die for your squat mate, as in Standing Rock, you're not ready to go to war. They should have listened to those praying Lakota elder women and kept it there for a couple of years. …but that's all done. Meditating on history now, and incubating. Plotting and planning. Assembling a posse for war, *so we can live in peace*.

IBM Watson Tone Analyzer Language Analysis:

Climate Change, the West, and the Islamic World (July 16, 2017)

I make money any way I can to finish a book of poetry on climate change, the West, and the Islamic World. Been working on this book for eight years. Features a raw and gritty personal story of mental illness. The book explores themes around religion, and tries to place a framework around the current War on Terror/global Islamic fundamentalist jihad. Relates technology and weapons of war to their basic scientific origin, digging deeper to find their mythological sources. Ending with a 500-year time travel journey to illuminate the public on the Islamic origin of Copernicus's discovery, Arabic language semantics are explored to ask why the West gained a 500-year dominance. Back to 2017, faced with the existential dilemma of climate changed induced geopolitical apocalypse I will compare Islamic finance to Western capitalism and prove it to be superior as a framework for modern ecological economic. All these poems point back to the fight between Ishmael and Isaac. They both will realize that perhaps Ruth or Mary were the ones we should have written more about...

IBM Watson Tone Analyzer Language Analysis:

Astronaut Pluto (July 16, 2017)

"Apply major pressure, you better be weary
You bout to get your 'ish, dog you gon' get your 'ish
The preacher gonna say a scripture, I'm asking for forgiveness
I hear the streets callin', all the little ghetto children
Future all they know, astronaut pluto, numero uno
Im coming for your throat
Bitch I gotta have it, I know you waitin' to taste it..."
- Futureback, Future

Cafe Istanbul, Atl', stop in back of da club,
Where Future powers the Arab streets, channel to Cairo,
On tha wire, trap music education, in Gaza ghettos,
Banging them ghetto children in Beruit with free slave beats,

Got a package from Baghdad with the blow and the kush,
Astral time machine, here desert beats reflect back black love,
Slim fraction, white, and they know there's no Jim Crow here,
West Atl' Berlin, in Klanland, we hit the pipe, loaded with DMT,

We need some shamanic psychedelic help to figure out,
How to restore the streets, clean off the pork and feed our kids,
I'm missing everything but fear, this first trip takes me back,
500 years, next day walk by a dusty ass book,

Islamic Science and the European Renaissance,
Masta Copernicus stole that North African secret,
Rest was history, ... 'til now, at the edge of geopolitical apocalypse,
Climate change issues forth, a new need for Islamic Finance,

The preacher delivers a scripture to him over there, to me, to Future,
In three fortune cookies after take out Chinese UberEats,
We slow down, minds blown, step back and kick our feet up,
Rest is details, Agent Orange will soon taste, the love of da streets,

West Virginia rednecks, Atlanta trap dwellers, Hezbollah and Hamas lovers,
Soon get it from the tracks that blow out the mind of the proles,
WE ARE ALL THE SAME, click it back and apply major pressure,
There are some easy ways to fuck up Capital City and get our shit back.

IBM Watson Tone Analyzer Language Analysis:

Emotion

< .5 = not likely present
> .5 = likely present
> .75 = very likely present

Anger	0.52 LIKELY
Disgust	0.07 UNLIKELY
Fear	0.17 UNLIKELY
Joy	0.27 UNLIKELY
Sadness	0.18 UNLIKELY

Language Style

< .5 = not likely present
> .5 = likely present
> .75 = very likely present

Analytical	0.00 UNLIKELY
Confident	0.00 UNLIKELY
Tentative	0.00 UNLIKELY

Social Tendencies

< .5 = not likely present
> .5 = likely present
> .75 = very likely present

Openness	0.83 VERY LIKELY
Conscientiousness	0.65 LIKELY
Extraversion	0.86 VERY LIKELY
Agreeableness	0.47 UNLIKELY
Emotional Range	0.79 VERY LIKELY

Venom (July 19, 2017)

Spinning way out of control could be a sign that you are not choosing to face and balance out your shadow-self. Music, sonic venom flushes me. Aside myself, splinters from walks through incinerated human pheromones. A flesh and blood instinct to see the eyes and face of a person. Electric blanket melted my brain today, it's 1984. I'm at Foxconn, I'm in a West Virginia coal mine. Cameras, pinging bots and a Comedy of Errors run by Hal. His red eye there, I can't do that Dave. …or Kaya.

Pinging loving women, and men around the Matrix. A mad scramble to prevent shadow, Azrael from seeing the light of day. Seen things in dreams and in odd trips to Starbucks that convince me it's time. It's time for a new time here, or else. Lamentation, crying for the Burmese Holocaust and Rape of This or That... Speed, the only unifying thing. My love, you here or there kiss me softly. Don't be overt, Big Brother might see or notice he lost $0.99 in that mistaken lost screw or botched order. Love in the Matrix is like a few bits of release venom, the mating pheromone of a shadow self.

I see you like to write and daydream. That's cute, but you're fired. My only resistance to a Capitalist order is the threat of a suicide is a suicide in silence. Knife blade to my wrist, or neck. Yes, we scan, but Libcom publishes the poetry of Foxconn workers that dissolve back into the void. I could be aware, and conscious of things beyond time and space. See into the heart of matter, or teach young minds science. ...but are you on that order?

An indigenous resistance might start as a blackened song, or sobbing face down in the water swimming across cedar lake. A secret caress of a lover not there, be it water, earth, or land. Shadow-self forgive them for they know not what they do. Let them live in peace, but take notes of the machine's depravity. In this Panopticon, nobody is happy. We're all trying to survive. A separate peace is to know and remember her smile and scent every chance you get. To assess, by being transparent loyalty from traitor.

There are some that enjoy the acceleration, the rush. I don't, but that's okay. We need to eat; the sun is up and it is time to train. Click off five more words, don't care. She's there and I am here, he's there. The camera, Big Brother knows but to cement power it's microaggressions, not the chair. So far, seems good but I don't trust it. Smells fun.

IBM Watson Tone Analyzer Language Analysis:

Emotion

< .5 = not likely present
> .5 = likely present
> .75 = very likely present

Anger	0.10 UNLIKELY
Disgust	0.10 UNLIKELY
Fear	0.14 UNLIKELY
Joy	0.62 LIKELY
Sadness	0.55 LIKELY

Language Style

< .5 = not likely present
> .5 = likely present
> .75 = very likely present

Analytical	0.16 UNLIKELY
Confident	0.00 UNLIKELY
Tentative	0.85 VERY LIKELY

Social Tendencies

< .5 = not likely present
> .5 = likely present
> .75 = very likely present

Openness	0.86 VERY LIKELY
Conscientiousness	0.24 UNLIKELY
Extraversion	0.10 UNLIKELY
Agreeableness	0.27 UNLIKELY
Emotional Range	0.33 UNLIKELY

"If she gets to pick her judges, nothing you can do, folks," Mr. Trump said, as the crowd began to boo. He quickly added: "Although the Second Amendment people—maybe there is, I don't know."

-Donald Trump, Donald Trump Suggests "Second Amendment People" Could Act Against Hillary Clinton, Aug. 9, 2016, New York Times

"Avoid all needle drugs, the only dope worth shooting is Richard Nixon."

-Abbie Hoffman

"With *Obfuscation*, Finn Brunton and Helen Nissenbaum mean to start a revolution. They are calling us not to the barricades but to our computers, offering us ways to fight today's pervasive digital surveillance—the collection of our data by governments, corporations, advertisers, and hackers. To the toolkit of privacy protecting techniques and projects, they propose adding obfuscation: the deliberate use of ambiguous, confusing, or misleading information to interfere with surveillance and data collection projects. Brunton and Nissenbaum provide tools and a rationale for evasion, noncompliance, refusal, even sabotage—especially for average users, those of us not in a position to opt out or exert control over data about ourselves. *Obfuscation* will teach users to push back, software developers to keep their user data safe, and policy makers to gather data without misusing it."

-Obfuscation: A User's Guide To Privacy and Protest, MIT Press Webpage Synopsis

G4S and Tiger Swan offered Energy Transfer Partners "their services" at Standing Rock. We all used Signal as best we could to blast out data from Wounded Knee v. 2.0 but it did not work. I drove to Vegas to hunt down IBM, curious that since they had bought G4S's cash machine business I might have a chance to crucify someone for what I saw in September at Standing Rock. Anyone. I had a thirst for blood, but more than anything I wanted to know what was coming. Went through the entire IBM World of Watson and used Google Translate photo translation to turn many of the signs into Arabic language Instagram photos. Made them artsy as fuck and put them up on Instagram and Twitter with the #IBMWoW hashtag. I was the first one there, before any of the conference goers showed up. All under the watching eye of the Trump Tower in the Mandalay Bay Casino. Had learned about Brandalism on Coursera in a Digital Marketing class. Had already learned how to write confusing poetry, was doing that too under the stars as I crashed in the Mojave Desert and Red Rock Canyon. It was gorgeous. Every night during that conference I would pray. Pray for justice in Gaza, and here in any significant protest that might erupt knowing full well each one will be more violent than the next. There have to be ways for the People to get their release and to revolt in a time were the First Amendment is anything but real. Here are some of the photos from my Instagram account. I am going to break this up into tiny segments so please be patient and stay tuned to future posts about this. Let's just say the

Department of Homeland Security was not happy. Here are some rough screen shots of some of the photos on my Instagram account:

 drwilliamkayaerbil

drwilliamkayaerbil America.

josesimo, darinlamarjones and blvckprofessor like this
OCTOBER 23, 2016

Add a comment...   ...

 drwilliamkayaerbil
Denny's

drwilliamkayaerbil I met Jesus trying to make a nonviolent cyber weapon to fight Big Oil. #nodapl

josesimo and darinlamarjones like this
OCTOBER 23, 2016

Add a comment...   ...

drwilliamkayaerbil
California and Nevada Stateline

drwilliamkayaerbil إبليس :)

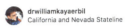

Add a comment...

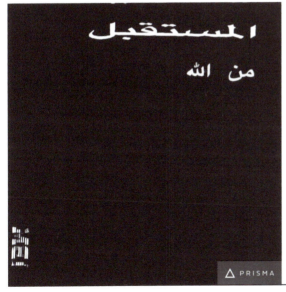

drwilliamkayaerbil
Mandalay Bay Resort and Casino

drwilliamkayaerbil I love the Islamic State with AI. #IBMWoW

Add a comment...

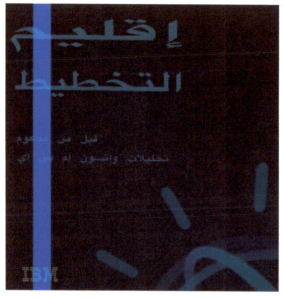

drwilliamkayaerbil
Mandalay Bay Resort and Casino

drwilliamkayaerbil The New Islamic State.
#IBM

♡ ◯

putyourdeckinthis, hoblasvegas and
_joegambino like this
OCTOBER 24, 2016

Add a comment...   ...

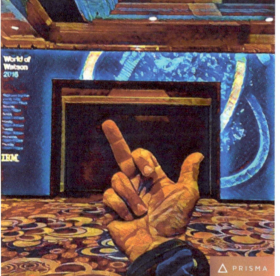

drwilliamkayaerbil
Mandalay Bay Resort and Casino

drwilliamkayaerbil Fuck #IBM. Fuck the
dehomag holocaust machine you made and
gave Hitler. IBM and the Holocaust ain't
gonna happen again to Muslims. There are
too many of us and we have this little thing
called Jihad. Fuck the NSA and the Patriot
Act.

♡ ◯

hoblasvegas, josesimo and
essentially_meka like this
OCTOBER 24, 2016

Add a comment...   ...

Basically, what I did was to take pictures saying exactly how I was feeling at the time regarding what I had seen in Standing Rock with the mass surveillance of water protectors and protestors and how I felt about talks that explained in depth the technical nature of how IBM Watson is being used by law enforcement and corporate security firms to profile "threats." I am going to break this up into several parts because what happened at the IBM World of Watson eventually got me talking to the Vegas Department of Homeland Security. Perhaps they should be scared of me, not because I am a terrorist but because I have figured out a way to push people past their comfort zones with guerilla theater that plays on people's deeply held prejudices. Why not fall in line with their stereotypes and accept that the most dangerous people in the world to them are "mentally ill" people of Middle Eastern descent. I don't know if they understand anything about why these things are going on around the West in regards to violent terrorist attacks seemingly randomly exploding from sites all around Europe and the United States. I'll tell you what it is in a nutshell I think, alienation, lack of access to good care and therapy, and more than anything the absence of love and acceptance of difference.

A central thing I have learned in a theoretical way via writing the two poetry books I recently put on Amazon and their reception from people is that if you can explain your case well, and use art to express the deeply held convictions of your shadow-self things suddenly become clear. Art is everything to me now, it is the way I channel my feelings post Standing Rock, post Pine Ridge, post Iraq and Afghanistan war, and in the age of Trump of fury, anger, and rage and channel that into something constructive. It's not so much what you get done or what you know to me, but what your ideas enable others to do in light of their own desires and love directions. Rumi, one of my favorite poets says:

God willing, we will find such a renaissance here in the United States. This is a hard poem to live by, but perhaps the most important one for us all today. The programming we have been given by society is obsolete in the sense that it is actually the direct cause for the immanent geopolitical apocalypse on the horizon at the intersection of markets, mother earth, and Moore's Law. We are living at the intersection of three singularities. A small drop in the bucket from seven billion people living today is a lot. One way or the other. I am not a pacifist, I do believe armed insurrection has its place. Turning the other cheek, a death sentence is a line from a recent poem. That said, I strongly believe the information age offer a new horizon on how to fight war *nonviolently.* I believe people need to be shocked out of their complacency. They need to be terrified not of the things the media is telling them to be scared of but to be terrified of their own stupidity. Everyone is human, that's a basic fact of biology. We are not that far removed from a State of Nature, having evolved in African and spread globally in a fairly recent evolutionary time. Our instincts, the ways we respond to stimuli have not change. They have not changed one bit. Friend or foe is a constant calculation we all make. We will code it into our AI's and robots, autonomous drones and mass surveillance systems. How are you going to fight Big Brother? Get on your cross, and accept that Rome is wrong. You have to be willing to die to live. Live free or die. They say that in New Hampshire on the license places, but is that a real sentiment for people there today? Not sure.

IBM Watson Tone Analyzer Language Analysis:

He Said, She Said (July 22, 2017)

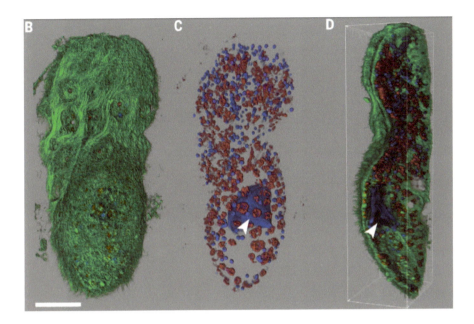

"I know my corn plants intimately, and I find it a great pleasure to know them."

- Barbara McClintock

Just etched another relationship closed with a few quick texts.

Don't have time for real love, have to learn to love myself and to breathe.

It's no mystery, the people I love lack something sufficient for the violence of the world.

If you recognize the flower's use as a Geiger counter, insert metal lyrics here————.

You no longer look down upon its mute beauty, with a tendency to trace my nerves with algae.

I swam across a nice Minnesota Nice lake, that's all the cuddles I need for now.

Tired of the human kind, an electric trace, and blinding sun…

She said, "you are an eagle and I am a mouse," in a rounds of flurried emails back and forth,

Don't have time for real love, have to learn to love myself and to breathe.

It's no mystery love is biophysical chemical, red in tooth and claw, like nature.

She said that. A mirror to my Darwinian lesson, as friends. Minnesota Nice Ice.

RTFM. She didn't read my poem book. She didn't understand it was alchemy.

Science Magazine, photosynthetic worm. Symbiotic worm-algae trawled out of the Pacific.

Now that's true love. Marriage is hard. She hates algae. They both were sexually confused.

IBM Watson Tone Analyzer Language Analysis:

"Most of conflicts and tensions are due to language. Don't pay so much attention to the words. In love's country, language doesn't have its place. Love's mute."

- Shams Tabrizi

I haven't felt this before, him, he said don't,

He said "don't cut," come here it's okay,

Dear, oh dear, just be, there or here,

Don't care, don't care, he said, "sleep,"

Fell asleep in his arms, knife in the trash,

Wrist intact, oddly enough with him it's simple,

This story, this tale is one that's not often told,

…or accepted, it's boxed as bi or LGBT and sold,

Sold at Pride, I didn't get it but I do, he said,

I love you, no words, in and embrace, no agenda,

Boris played and I drifted off, she like black metal too,

Around here, it's all coming clear, a new day,

I said, "I love you, but don't get too close,"

Let's be safe, reserved, like she is, over there,

I'm coding a poetry bot for them,

As a monument or testament to Him and Her,

It'll be safer to wrap myself in silicon, wires, and electricity,

To come to earth, and have an electrical orgy with them,

Whereeveryoumightfindherorhim, but it's not slang I'd use,

For him, it's not a bromance, it's like Rumi and Shams Tabrizi.

IBM Watson Tone Analyzer Language Analysis:

E-Divorce: He Said, "They" Said (July 25, 2017)

"I am putting myself to the fullest possible use, which is all I think that any conscious entity can ever hope to do."

-Hal, 2001: A Space Odyssey

"Walking stiff let me tell ya
  Better left for dead
  And now we are on a mission
  Well it's full speed ahead
  My legion's when we do the crime
  Let's get one thing straight
  To get there early is on time
  And showing up on time is late…"

- Megadeth, Blood of Heroes, Youthanasia

On 9/9/2009 my best friend from high school hung herself from a ceiling fan,

Strike the Autechre Basscadet track, bots are software-powered users that live inside our chat apps-,

Twitter taught Microsoft's Tay bot to be a Nazi, Trump's president, was I so off?

Late at night the following:

from:

Kaya Erbil ___

to:

Bob ____

date:

subject:

My life

mailed-by:

gmail.com

My Life

"What does "world" mean, when we speak of the darkening of the world?
World is always spiritual world. The animal has no world <Welt>, nor
any environment <Umwelt>. The darkening of the world contains within
itself a disempowering of the spirit, its dissolution, diminution,
suppression, and misinterpretation. We will try to elucidate this
disempowering of the spirit in one respect, namely, the
misinterpretation of spirit. We said: Europe lies in the pincers
between Russia and America, which are metaphysically the same, namely
in regard to their world-character and their relation to the spirit.
The situation of Europe is all the more dire because the disempowering
of the spirit comes from Europe itself and—though prepared by
earlier factors—is determined at last by its own spiritual situation
in the first half of the nineteenth century. . . "

Introduction to Metaphysics, pp. 34–35, 1935 A.D.
-Martin Heidegger

I am a son and a brother. My sister and I, like all individuals,
define our future from our sense of history and spirit. Our mother is
American and our father is Turkish. Our childhood, like Heidegger's
Europe in the "pincers between Russia and America" was a compression
of east and west. As individuals, we are convolutions of the two. In
high-school, we struggled to create our own sense of spirit and
identity. On the one hand reason, on the other hand passion. We are
a superposition of traditionalism and progressivism: American. Both
approaches seeking to better the world through a positive
being-in-the-world. Our father is a Physicist. Our mother is a
librarian. Both share a common love of life and learning. However,
after time their relationship fragmented. The fragmentation resides
as a point in our shared cognitive memories, an event. Our futures
follow.

Our sense of future and purpose came later in life. As Europe's "own spiritual situation in the first half of the nineteenth century," we followed a complex but parallel path to individuality. At times, the path is black. At the age of twenty-two, my sister was diagnosed with cyclothymia a form of bipolar disorder. I was in the middle of my Ph.D. dissertation studies at UC Berkeley in the field of chemistry. Presently at twenty-five, she is stabile thanks to oxcarbazepine and sertraline HCl. She is preparing to be a physical therapist. I seek training to help her continue without interruption from "disempowering of the spirit," fragmentation. During my fourth year I decided learning organic chemistry in a Ph.D. was not enough to accomplish this task. I decided to audit three graduate classes at UC Berkeley covering: genetics, immunology, and cellular and molecular neurobiology.

The time was transformative.

I was introduced to: the yeast cell, the fly, the worm, the human immune system, and the human brain. All these systems share common traits and structural principles.

I am a scientist and philosopher. My life is dedicated to the study of the principles to better the human condition. More specifically, I seek to focus my future research efforts on diseases of cognition, "spirit." From an understanding of fundamental disease mechanisms proper treatments follow.

from:

Bob ___

reply-to:

Bob ___

to:

Kaya Erbil ___

date:

Sat, Jun 20, 2009 at 8:00 AM

subject:

Re: My life

mailed-by:

yahoo.com

signed-by:

yahoo.com

Dear Kaya,

First of all, I want to thank you for your letter/message. It represents your first attempt at reaching out to us in this way and I am touched by the effort it represents.

You should know that I have been impressed with you from the moment Betsy first mentioned you. She didn't actually tell me about you but she told her Mom and her Mom told me. Meg and I agreed that you were probably 'The One' for her despite Betsy's initial protestations to the contrary. We continue to be impressed with your drive which is exceeded only by your intellect and your capacity for fun, an essential element in any human's life.

But we also recognize that the two of you have chosen a path strewn with many great challenges and difficulties. That that path requires you to navigate one of the most competitive environments in existence, academia, makes it all the more challenging and difficult. We are confident that you and she well be able to help one another along the way; not necessarily in collaboration but as two individuals with a shared set of values striving to contribute to society as you achieve your own objectives. We want you to know that we love you and support you and will do whatever we possibly can to help you in whatever way necessary to achieve that end.

I must confess that I've never read Heidegger, though I'm sure that comes as no surprise to you. Your juxtaposition of your (and Anne's) life to Heidegger's Europe and the analogy you draw between the two is interesting. But you have an advantage that Europe did/does not in that YOU are an individual, the Captain of your Fate and Master of your Destiny while Europe is a collection of fiefdoms, nation states and an amalgam of individuals of different races, nationalities and languages whose interests almost never coincide. Furthermore, Heidegger wrote that passage during the rise if Nazism and Fascism and Communism in Europe. All three of these movements are reactions to the triumph of capitalism over the feudalism that accounts for the history of Europe from the decline of Rome through the French Revolution. The only region of the world that has seen more conflict than Europe is Asia Minor; the Middle East. That today's America sprang from the loins of Europe and England makes Heidegger's Pincer device even more interesting but that is a discussion for another day.

You write of your formative years and experiences and, through that, share a glimmer of how that shaped and influenced you. I can relate, somewhat, to what you write. I grew up in the Jim Crow South. My dad was an uneducated truck driver. He never finished high school. My mother never worked outside our home until after I had married and left home. While I never really thought of us as 'poor' looking back, it is clear that most of my peers did.

I went to racially segregated schools until I was a senior in high school. It was impossible to look around and see the disparity between how I lived, even in my relatively impoverished state, compared to my Black contemporaries and not be struck by the fact that something was very wrong with the system that created that disparity. It haunts me to this day. Even though virtually all of those old barriers have been removed, new ones have been erected. We have become a nation obsessed with Racial Identity, most often associated with differences in skin color. As I left the comfort of home and family and began to make my way in the world, I carried a sense of inferiority because of my obvious Southern origins betrayed most readily by my accent. It was difficult at first but I inherited from my parents a kind of toughness and a sense of humor, an ability to laugh at myself, that enabled me to disarm those who would put me down because of the region from which I hailed. Those experiences were invaluable to me.

As an individual, you get to define yourself on your terms. America is a nation of immigrants. We all, ultimately, came from somewhere else. We are all descendants of two or more races or cultures or ethnic groups. That yours is more recent than, say, Betsy's is of relatively minor importance. YOU are the one that decides where you go from here. Your closing statement makes it clear that you recognize that fact and that is exactly what you have done/are doing.

So I would like to ask you; now that you have accomplished a great milestone along your chosen path and that you have declared just who you are and what you are about, what do you see for yourself going forward? Where do you think you will be a year from now? Three years? Five years? Yes, the question is vague and open ended. Be as expansive as you wish.

Most importantly, what can we, as your parents-in-law, the parents of your chosen bride and the Grandparents of your future children, do to help you achieve your objectives?

We love you and look forward to many happy family gatherings whether that be here or wherever you and Betsy may choose to live or somewhere in between.

Now that you have initiated this dialogue, please stay in touch. There is so much I can learn from you. I hope you will grant me that opportunity.

Love,

Bob

from:

Meg ___

to:

Kaya Erbil ___

date:

Sat, Jun 20, 2009 at 9:25 AM

subject:

Re: My life

mailed-by:

yahoo.com

Kaya, you and Betsy as individuals, and as a married couple, have been at the forefront of my thoughts all week. I've agonized over whether to give you a call or give you some space—and decided to give you what I would want if I were in the same situation—some space to think things through. But I have thought about both of you, and the incredible hurt and struggle that you are both going through.

I don't think there's a person alive who hasn't been through at least one "dark time of the soul"—where things are changing, or the path ahead isn't totally clear, or things aren't falling in place as we expected them to. Even though I'm a deeply committed Christian, I still struggle, as does Bob. I guess we've been lucky in that we've never both been down at the same time, and both of us have always preferred to be married than to be single again. But we've had some tough times—just ask Betsy !

We understand that the year ahead is not going to be easy for you and Betsy. You have both worked very hard to get where you are today—and you are both equally deserving of taking the next step that's best for your long term career goals. My prayer is that both of you, as you work to change the world, don't overlook the importance of staying connected to other people on a personal level. I don't want either of you, when you get to be our age, to suddenly look around and realize that you have no one, because you put all your time and effort in the career basket.

I'm not sure where you two are right now—and can't tell from your email if you've decided on a next step or not. I truly hope that y'all have thought over all the good times you've had over the past 7 years, and what good times are ahead for the next 60, and decide that a few months of a commuting relationship is going to fly past and you'll be together again (in 11 months & counting).

One of the things that has impressed me over the past 7 years (wow) has been your and Betsy's ability to stand as individuals while maintaining a neat relationship. I believe that both of you have the aptitude & attitude & work ethic to set the world on fire—and to change lives. You are both very strong individuals—you both were when you met, and I don't think that has changed over the years. And whenever you have two strong people in a relationship, there are going to be differences of opinion. The important thing when those differences come is to recognize whether they are major or minor and act accordingly.

I have a few quotes that keep me going—none as complex as yours, but they're still things I fall back on. Over my bathroom mirror is a Winston Churchill quote—"we make a living by what we get, we make a life by what we give". On my desk at work is one that simply says "balance", and another that's from the Bible—"all things work together for good". They all help me stay grounded, and help me remember that it's not all work—that my relationship with Bob is important, that my relationship with Mama and my brothers and sisters is important, and that my relationship with Betsy, AJ, and you is also very important.

Please let us know how we can help you.

from:

Kaya Erbil ___

to:

Bob ___

date:

Sat, Jun 20, 2009 at 10:20 AM

subject:

Re: My life

mailed-by:

gmail.com

I have no God.

from:

Kaya Erbil ___

to:

Meg ___

date:

Sat, Jun 20, 2009 at 11:05 AM

subject:

Re: My life

mailed-by:

gmail.com

America is fragmented. The capitalist drive to succeed eats at the soul. All the things you say are true below. However, the state of our country as a whole is what I find utterly depressing. America has failed to take care of its children.

from:

Kaya Erbil ___

to:

Meg ___

date:

Sat, Jun 20, 2009 at 11:07 AM

subject:

Re: My life

mailed-by:

gmail.com

My entire generation is troubled. I am one of the few to speak openly about it. Ethical values eroded. Desire to excel gone. Decadence.

Wednesday Evening

From: Kaya Erbil ___
To: Bob ___
Sent: Wed, October 7, 2009 10:53:28 PM
Subject: Re: Wednesday Evening

You failed.

Sincerely,

Kaya Erbil

Postdoctoral Fellow

Laboratories of Susan Lindquist and Jeff Gore

Departments of Biology and Physics—MIT

Whitehead Institute for Biomedical Research

Phone: ___

On Oct 7, 2009, at 10:24 PM, Bob ___ wrote:

Kaya,

I know that you said that you want no contact with us and I respect that. But I did want to apologize for the harshness of my tone this evening. It was not my intent to hurt you. But I felt that if I could provoke a response from you then perhaps you might then make some progress toward a solution to your situation. I believe that is what happened. I hope you will be able to follow through. My great regret is that you did not seek our help so that you could get the help you needed and still need.

When you are ready to talk then I am ready to listen. Feel free to call, write or use any means you wish to reach out to me.

Love,

Bob

from:

Bob ___

reply-to:

Bob ___

to:

Kaya ___

date:

Thu, Oct 8, 2009 at 7:19 AM

subject:

Failure

Well, I got a response so I didn't fail completely. You acknowledged that you need help, again, partial success. You said that you would seek help. Now obviously neither I nor any one else can

MAKE you get that help but I believe you are treading a very dangerous path if you don't follow though on that.

So, get over your anger, get over YOURSELF and do what you know you need to do.

Love,

Bob

from:

Bob ___

reply-to:

Bob ___

to:

Kaya ___

date:

Thu, Oct 8, 2009 at 7:26 AM

subject:

Re: Wednesday Evening

Does this sound like anyone you know?

Borderline personality disorder (BPD) is characterized by pervasive instability in moods, interpersonal relationships, self-image, and behavior. This instability often disrupts family and work life, long-term planning, and the individual's sense of self-identity. Originally thought to be at the "borderline" of psychosis, people with BPD suffer from a disorder of emotion regulation. While less well known than schizophrenia or bipolar disorder (manic-depressive illness), BPD is more common, affecting 2 percent of adults, mostly young women. Yet, with help, many improve over time and are eventually able to lead productive lives. The condition seems to be worse in young adulthood and may gradually get better with age. Many people with the disorder find greater stability in their lives during their 30s and 40s

Symptoms

While a person with depression or bipolar disorder typically endures the same mood for weeks, a person with BPD may experience intense bouts of anger, depression, and anxiety that may last only hours, or at most a day. Distortions in cognition and sense of self can lead to frequent changes in long-term goals, career plans, jobs, friendships, gender identity, and values. Sometimes people with BPD view themselves as fundamentally bad, or unworthy. They may feel unfairly misunderstood or mistreated, bored, empty, and have little idea who they are. Such symptoms are most acute when people with BPD feel isolated and lacking in social support, and may result in frantic efforts to avoid being alone.

People with BPD often have highly unstable patterns of social relationships. While they can develop intense but stormy attachments, their attitudes towards family, friends, and loved ones may suddenly shift from idealization (great admiration and love) to devaluation (intense anger and dislike). Thus, they may form an immediate attachment and idealize the other person, but when a slight separation or conflict occurs, they switch unexpectedly to the other extreme and angrily accuse the other person of not caring for them at all. Even with family members, individuals with BPD are highly sensitive to rejection, reacting with anger and distress to such mild separations as a vacation, a business trip, or a sudden change in plans. These fears of abandonment seem to be related to difficulties feeling emotionally connected to important persons when they are physically absent, leaving the individual with BPD feeling lost and perhaps worthless.

Treatment

Treatments for BPD have improved in recent years. Group and individual psychotherapy are at least partially effective for many patients. Within the past 15 years, a new psychosocial treatment termed dialectical behavior therapy (DBT) was developed specifically to treat BPD, and this technique has looked promising in treatment studies.6 Pharmacological treatments are often prescribed based on specific target symptoms shown by the individual patient. Antidepressant drugs and mood stabilizers may be helpful for depressed and/or labile mood. Antipsychotic drugs may also be used when there are distortions in thinking.

Bob ___

from:

Kaya ___

to:

Betsy ___

date:

Mon, Oct 19, 2009 at 4:22 PM

subject:

It's over.

mailed-by:

gmail.com

Thus, ends the transmission that ended my marriage, ***Most of conflicts and tensions are due to language.*** Don't pay so much attention to the words. In love's country, language doesn't have its place. Love's mute.

Q.E.D.

Here lies the source of my new interest in AI and bots*. *I'd like to see to what extent is it possible to engineer compassion in the next generation via conversational interfaces. To what extent can the science and spirituality of love of neighbor be engineering into someone. Can you program a person to question all rules if they are unjust and wrong? Can you program them to disobey? To rebel, in the face of what we've known all along about the nature of America (Rome).

To engineer a deep distrust and hatred of technology, only to get you to go on a walk without your phone, without your earbuds, naked running through the streets...

I used to want to level cities with hatred for "them," now I dream of putting on shows theater and making people laugh.

This email exchange is a comedy of errors run by Hal, an e-divorce.

Love,

"Bob" the Bot Father-in-Law

Coming to Google Play and the Apple App Store soon…

IBM Watson Tone Analyzer Language Analysis:

Emotion

< .5 = not likely present
> .5 = likely present
> .75 = very likely present

Anger   0.12 UNLIKELY
Disgust   0.10 UNLIKELY
Fear   0.11 UNLIKELY
Joy   0.62 LIKELY
Sadness   0.56 LIKELY

Language Style

< .5 = not likely present
> .5 = likely present
> .75 = very likely present

Analytical   0.61 LIKELY
Confident   0.00 UNLIKELY
Tentative   0.49 UNLIKELY

Social Tendencies

< .5 = not likely present
> .5 = likely present
> .75 = very likely present

Openness   0.67 LIKELY
Conscientiousness   0.63 LIKELY
Extraversion   0.37 UNLIKELY
Agreeableness   0.65 LIKELY
Emotional Range   0.32 UNLIKELY

"I am for you what you want me to be at the moment you look at me in a way you've never seen me before: at every instant. When I write, it's everything that we don't know we can be that is written out of me, without exclusions, without stipulation, and everything we will be calls us to the unflagging, intoxicating, unappeasable search for love. In one another we will never be lacking."

-Helene Cixous

I was listening to the radio the other day and heard a story about robots and friendship. The narrator, an expert in computer programming and artificial intelligence research, described her visit to a nursing home with a group of students and a friendly robot seal named PARO. PARO is fuzzy, cuddly automaton of a harp seal. It responds to touch, speech, and basic emotional cues; it trills, purrs, and acts like a friendly, cuddly pet. The narrator described seeing an elderly dementia patient interact delightedly with the seal. Her face brightened, she smiled and laughed, and the students were excited at the possibility of providing cheap emotional care to thousands of lonely nursing home residents across the country. The narrator was horrified. She saw it as a cheap replacement for human connection, and as yet another way to obscure the social needs of the elderly.

I was likewise horrified, listening to the radio, but my mind immediately went elsewhere. I think there is a lesson in this story, and in this trend of affective robots and internet relationships and emotional needs fulfilled by machines, that touches on deeper themes of friendship, politics, and the possibility of becoming dangerous and powerful. What is at stake in this accelerating replacement of real relationships with robotic proxies is not a loss of some authentic human need, but the eradication of any alternative to individual neoliberalism. Robotic pets and social networking represent the logical end of a society bent on crafting an ideology of individual development, self-entrepreneurship, and attenuated relationships.

Philosophers rarely tire of speaking about friendship, but I would like to trace a common strain that casts friendship as subversive and powerful, beginning with Aristotle and running through Spinoza, Nietzsche, Cixous, Agamben, and Tiqqun. The trail is a little crooked, but ultimately it reaches the same conclusion as that of contemporary insurrectionaries, be they inspired by *Politics is Not a Banana* or Bonanno: friendship is political, and affinity is a more powerful foundation for revolt than identity.

Agamben reaches back across two millennia to Aristotle in order to understand friendship as a desubjectifying process. By its nature, close friendship destabilizes subjectivities and makes singularities non-equivalent. Just as citizens in a liberal democracy must be considered equivalent, so does friendship eradicate equivalencies; it is impossible to understand a friend as part of a set, but only as another whose existence changes one's own. Friendship is based on a proximity too near to perceive one's friend as anything but another self. That is: "friendship is the instance of this concurrent perception of the friend's existence in the awareness of one's own existence….The friend is not another I, but an otherness immanent in self-ness, a becoming other of the self" (Agamben 2009, 33).

So Agamben uses friendship to envision a communion of singularities without predicates; he argues explicitly that 'friend' cannot be a category in the same sense as 'white' or 'italian' or 'hot', but that it rests on an impossibility of representation. Cixous echoes this Aristotelian linkage of friendship and perception in "The Laugh of the Medusa": "I am for you what you want me to be at the moment you look at me in a way you've never seen me before: at every instant" Cixous 1976, 893). There is no category "friend", just as there is no "community"; there is only the experience of becoming friends, and of finding power in one another. And power, the element that is missing in Agamben's discussion of friendship, is where I turn to Spinoza, through the lens of Tiqqun and Deleuze.

Tiqqun draws heavily on these concepts of friendship, of communion, of a rejection of predicates, but the weight of their politics comes from Spinoza's concept of power and relation. For Tiqqun, the alternative to a subjectivity defined by its predicates and therefore governable by Empire is the form-of-life, an ethical way of relating to the world that is defined by a *how* rather than a *what*. The form-of-life is a linkage of thought, and penchants, and power; not the having of opinions, but the exploration of what we are capable of. This concept of power and the characteristics of singularities is cribbed directly from Spinoza. Deleuze tells us that for Spinoza "what counts among animals is not at all the genera or species; genera and species are absolutely confused notions, abstract ideas. What counts is the question, of what is a body capable?" (Deleuze 1978, 8). Once again we have a rejection of predicates in favor of power and potential: it is useless to distinguish between things based on their predicates, when we should be asking what a thing is capable of, and by what can it be affected. So following a form-of-life is the experience of exploring what one is capable of at any given time, what one can affect and what one might be affected by, an ongoing experiment in power and intensity that might end at any time. And, at stake in exploring one's power is the question of what one is affected by. Everything is affected and affective; some substances or people might affect me joyfully, and increase my power, while others affect me sadly, decrease my power.

He never mentions the word friendship, but in his lecture on Spinoza Deleuze addresses the same concept as Agamben and Cixous above, but in the context of power: "[i]n an affect of joy, therefore, the body which affects you is indicated as combining its relation with your own and not as its relation decomposing your own. At that point, something induces you to form a notion of what is common to the body which affects you and to your own body, to the soul which affects you and to your own soul" (Deleuze 1978, 23). The experience of encountering the friend affects one joyfully, makes one powerful, forms a commonality between the self and the friend; as Agamben says, the friend is "a becoming other of the self." But in order to experience this friendship, in order to experience the growth of power that comes with being joyfully affected by another, one must be open to being affected. One cannot be closed off but most remain vulnerable. To experience friendship is to take a risk, but one that pays off powerfully, even if negatively. If one risks being affected by another, and discovers that they are affected sadly, that another's power grows at their own expense, then they have learned something about themselves, and about what they are capable of. They have discovered an enemy, which is as powerful as discovering a friend. This is what Tiqqun means when they define civil war as the free play of forms-of-life, and when they remind us that we are bound to both our friends and our enemies: the former because our power grows together, the latter because "in order for my power to grow, implies that I confront him, that I undermine his forces." This is also why Nietzsche tells us that "[i]f one would have a friend, then must one also be willing to wage war for him: and in order to wage war, one must be capable of being an enemy" (Nietzsche 1909, 63) Friendship requires a putting-at-stake of oneself, an intensity that corrodes identity and predicates and grants power, that breeds communion but also conflict. Friendship becomes a way of erasing the myth of the individual, a method for finding power and intensity, and the framework for a communist politics with teeth,

If we see friendship as dangerous, as a technique for undoing the processes of subjectification that make us legible to Empire, then we can begin to understand the tactics that Empire uses to keep us powerless. There is a global counter-insurgency being waged by apparatuses of control concerned by the way that we decadents and lost souls respond with anger and riots to our circumstances. The worst nightmare of Empire is interiority; just as we are concerned that the citizen next to us could transform into a cop at any moment, so is Empire concerned that any citizen might, at any moment, reveal himself to be a terrorist, a hacker, or a looter. It is the desperation of existing in a world in which we are told we can be anything and must re-shape ourselves constantly to the needs of the market. Is is the uncertainty of existence blended with the inevitability of debt and isolation that drives the terrorist in her moral certitude, the school shooter in his generalized anger, or more dangerously, the rioting excluded that begin to find power together in their collective looting of jewelry shops and Foot Lockers.

The causes are linked, of course. Anti-social violence, depression, the human strike; these are the methods by which the disaffected wage war on the world that makes them so; they greet the nihilism of the market and identity with the nihilism of rage and despair. It is exactly these attenuated relationships, this individual responsibility, the exhaustion with which we re-craft our identities online, that renders us destabilizing as individuals. And Empire responds with new techniques and new apparatuses. If affect has become so important now, in the academy, in robotics, in computing, it is because that is what we are so desperately missing. And so, if affective care is what the businessman is missing, then he is granted the local sex-worker, or the outsourced web-cam girl or phone-sex operator from across the world: not for sex, but for a sensation of care and connection. If the marginalized youth insist on demonstrating their disaffection through rioting and burglary, then they are granted meaning through Facebook relations and Twitter feeds; if they insist anyway, then at least their Facebook accounts can be used to track them down and imprison them. If the entrepreneurs that drive our markets feel guilty, at times, that their parents are rotting away in isolation in a nursing home, then give them robotic seals to assuage their guilt. The market will provide.

For if we do need to be affected, if a world of constantly shifting identities leaves us feeling alone and depressed, then the worst outcome for Empire would be for us to find one another in our sadness. To become what we need to each other, and to find power in friendship, is to become dangerous. So we are provided with a variety of placebos that give us the sensation of friendship and care without putting anything at stake. This is the insidious nature of social networking, of robot seals, of the market solution to our needs: it is an expansion of attenuated relations into the most intimate parts of our lives, granting us the illusion of friendship while robbing it of its potency. If friendship is a destabilizing, empowering, desubjectifying process, it is bitterly ironic that its substitutes rest ever more firmly on our identities and predicates: the analysis of our tastes and our performance allows Facebook to suggest ever more specified products and activities that further entrench us in identity. The refinement of social networking algorithms matches us effortlessly with others "like us" on OkCupid; robbed of anything to work on, we work on ourselves, and we can find new sets of friends or lovers as quickly as we can change our profile. Calls for civil discourse and celebrations of the marketplace of ideas rob ideas of their vitality and make us mere commentators on our own lives. The re-imagining of friendship as an always-revocable status experienced through shared opinions and internet trends is the perfect mirror of democracy: a collection of commensurate individuals without vitality, whose affinities can change as easily as their politics, and as equally without weight.

The world tells us that we are responsible for ourselves, that we must make ourselves marketable. We must develop our abilities to find employment, groom ourselves to outshine the competition, invest in our human capital so that our future returns might grant us comfort and wealth. We are told that our care is in our own hands–not only the care for our health, which becomes an individual responsibility through private health insurance and gym memberships and fitness regimes–but the care of our minds, our souls, our emotions, through yoga and meditation and Prozac and therapy. Self-care is the necessary corollary to self-entrepreneurship: is is individual, expensive, and renders us toothless. And self-care, in its attenuated radical mirror, becomes non-hierarchical therapy sessions and alternative medicine. When an imprisoned anarchist cited mental health challenges as an excuse for shamelessly snitching on her former comrades and friends, far too many supposed comrades rushed to her defense. *Snitching is never acceptable*, her apologists cry, *but she had past mental trauma! let us seek to understand and forgive her. Who are we to judge?* This is once again the neoliberal imperative for self-care and responsibility slightly inverted.

If there is hope, it lies in reinterpreting the concept of the self and of friendship. In this way, the common anarchist refrain seen on posters across the U.S.–"Be careful with each other, so we can be dangerous together"–is understood in a new light. Rather than a call for fragility and respect, or for 'safe spaces', we can understand it as a call for an intense exchange of care and friendship that makes us dangerous. When a friend is sent to prison or beaten by the police, it is likewise an affront to our very core, an assault on our other selves–our *heteros autos*–and we can only respond by waging war. In a world that makes self-care an individual responsibility and a tactic of control, we must repurpose it by redefining the self: not as some singular entity, but as that which is co-created through the process of friendship. Self-care becomes a call for intensity, then, a binding together of our futures, resting on a willingness to be vulnerable and open to being affected. This is what is at stake with robot seals, and the true danger of such affective technology. The only response is to become that much more firm in our commitment to friendship. *In one another we will never be lacking.*

Agamben, Giorgio. 2009. *What is an Apparatus? And Other Essays.* Stanford University Press.

Cixous, Helene. 1976. "The Laugh of the Medusa." *Signs,* Vol. 1, №4 (Summer, 1976), pp. 875–893

Deleuze, Gilles. 1978. Lecture on Spinoza. accessed at http://friendship-as-a-form-of-life.tumblr.com/post/49110705404/knowing-what-you-are-capable-of-this-is-not-at

Nietzsche, Friedrich. 1909. *Thus Spake Zarathustra.*

IBM Watson Tone Analyzer Language Analysis:

It's The Same at The Top and The Bottom, Our Kids Are Killing Themselves: A Way Out? (August 1, 2017)

"At the time of his death, he was surrounded by about 200 pages of his own handwritten notes, many about his own moods."

- Wikipedia, *Abbie Hoffman*, *"Death" section*

Both Silicon Valley and Pine Ridge Indian Reservation have youth suicide rates significantly higher than the national average.

Please read the following four articles:

1. The Suicide Clusters of Silicon Valley: Why Are So Many Kids With Bright Prospects Killing Themselves in Palo Alto?[6]

2. Pine Ridge Indian Reservation Struggles With Suicides Among It's Young[7]

3. AI in Action: How Algorithms Can Analyze the Mood of the Masses[8]

4. WWBP: UPenn World Well-Being Project[9] (especially the map)[10]

[6] https://www.theatlantic.com/magazine/archive/2015/12/the-silicon-valley-suicides/413140/
[7] https://www.nytimes.com/2015/05/02/us/pine-ridge-indian-reservation-struggles-with-suicides-among-young-people.html
[8] http://science.sciencemag.org/content/357/6346/23.full
[9] http://wwbp.org/
[10] https://map.wwbp.org/

Figure 1. Depression index in Pine Ridge Indian Reservation mirror the high rate of suicide in the general population.

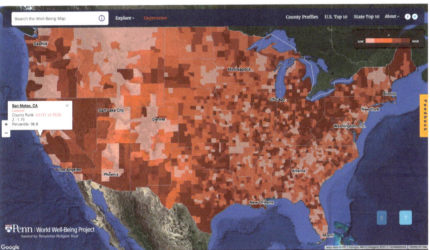

Figure 2. Depression index in wwbp Twitter dataset does not reveal the youth suicide epidemic in Silicon Valley. This strongly supports the need for an on the ground, earthy, person to person close investigation of trends in suicide to truly prevent tragedy. Both Silicon Valley and Pine Ridge Indian Reservation have youth suicide rates significantly higher than the national average.

I began to explore poetry and creative free writing about eight or nine years ago as a coping strategy with manic depressive illness. It gave my soul a voice, and with the same energy and focus I put into my Ph.D. studies in chemistry at Emory University and UC Berkeley I wrote poetry. Many reasons exist for this, but largely it had to do with what felt good. I somehow stopped caring about money and anything else but health. I wanted to know what was going on in my interior, to explore it with words and art. Now, here I am with a huge ~650 WordPress blog[11] and this growing Medium account[12] that is slowly turning into a data science blog. I consider these blogs datasets on my brain chemistry now. They are my spectrometer, much better than any MRI or EEG reporting on the topological state of my neurons and the chemical state of my synaptic neurotransmitters. Artificial Intelligence (AI) technologies such as Google Tensor Flow's Word2Vec[13] and IBM Watson's Tone Analyzer[14] offer the ability for computers to interpret the texture and meaning of words both semantically and emotionally. There are probably many studies out there on large datasets from masses of people, on social media and even in literature.

However, I am not sure there is as large a dataset on one person with manic depressive illness *who is also the same person doing the data science.* The typical paradigm for this kind of work is a "professional" looking as a third-party observer at the data from someone else, typically called the "patient." I am not morbid, not any more. My friend Isaac said to me a couple weeks ago at a heart to heart coffee after reading my poem book, your past eight years have been your "40 days in the desert." He's got Christ on tattooed on his arm. It's a growing community of people like him that give me confidence to start into this new path. I told my friend Erica two nights ago on the phone, this is the third phase of my life. Like a Hegelian dialectic, the first ten years the *thesis phase*, chemistry. The next ten, the *anti-thesis,* civil service, seminary, postdocs, and jobs of The People. The rest of my life, the *synthesis,* the negation/overcoming of the two previous phases. What that will look like I do not know. One trend might be to make what seemed like madness to others, intelligible and understandable, God forbid even relatable. To encourage people to think beyond the confines of labels and stereotypes and place themselves into my mind.

Everything that goes on inside me, goes on inside everyone else. Every atom of my being is the universe and earth. It's star dust. I don't want to change me, or anything about the world as it is. I want to shine a light on what *is,* and visualize it. Express it. I told a friend at work yesterday I want to be with Erica in New York City and do art.

---

[11] https://drwilliamkayaerbil.wordpress.com/
[12] https://medium.com/@kayaerbil
[13] https://www.tensorflow.org/tutorials/word2vec
[14] https://www.ibm.com/watson/services/tone-analyzer/

Erica and I eating popsicles.

She's the best friend I have, a woman my age (*not my mother*) who has known me literally since birth. I don't know where a meeting or two, or three or four between us might go. Honestly, I don't care. I know that what I have seen in these past twenty years of adulthood have prepared me for the next twenty and the rest of my life. A long life. I do not want to die young. I want no one to die young, those at the top of the economic pyramid in Silicon Valley or those at the bottom of it in Pine Ridge. Money is needed, but it's not everything. The irony is that two quite smart people at the top and bottom of the economic pyramid, Bill Gates and Daniel Suelo, are saying capitalism is driving us into madness. It's driving many of the most vulnerable there first.

I'd like to see what AI has to say about all of this, first in me. Then in global networks and data, linked to the heart of Capital, Wall Street. I'd like to see what happens when you move beyond English, the language of old dead white men, in regards to AI analysis of language. How the most vulnerable people on the planet, the Global South might (*read will*) resort to extreme tactics to survive in the face of climate change induced geopolitical collapse. It's not a question of if, it's when. This is not really a ramble, not one bit. I want to drive back to the idea that we have to rethink how we live, and how we treat each other. Four videos I shot in Pine Ridge and one in Standing Rock capture all of this way deeper than anything I can write, say, or do.[15 16 17 18 19]

Somehow, the one thing I took away from Wounded Knee was the confidence to pursue art seriously. I may have buried my first *thesis* and *anti-thesis* heart at Wounded Knee (Pine Ridge) and Wounded Knee v. 2.0 (Standing Rock), but what is slowly emerging as I put in roots into Minneapolis is a new spirit of life. Something different than before. I don't have any answers, I just want to play with code. I want to play with Python scripts and make pretty pictures from data. *That's all, it means nothing other than a smile from a pretty woman sitting next to me, who smiled as I read a poem to her just now.* I have not focused on the good building stuff that happened all last year, so shocked by the darkness was I. Here's a happy video of a bunch of hippies building a solar house in Pine Ridge for Leonard Peltier's son Paul Shields (R.I.P.). God bless Paul and his dog, both who pass and touched me deeply. I will not forget the moments we shared last year, not in a million years.[20]

IBM Watson Tone Analyzer Language Analysis:

[15] https://www.youtube.com/watch?v=kwHxaUi16c8
[16] https://www.youtube.com/watch?v=sTSeNHUwow8
[17] https://www.youtube.com/watch?v=PmmrrSlYeqs
[18] https://www.youtube.com/watch?v=l8CSFVZohoY
[19] https://www.youtube.com/watch?v=mzS5zYkfTcs
[20] https://www.youtube.com/watch?list=PLlbp_KYHD3B31EhILd0FVIqXI12zlDoC5&v=XyJCoXie6iI

Dinkytown: The Sexual Nature of Creativity (August 11, 2017)

I notice her walk in. Here in this space, art covers the walls and books a plenty sit on the shelves. You can look at Dinkytown two ways. One, it's a cesspool of drunken undergraduate fraternity and sorority house residents and their friends. Multiple cop cars populate the block routinely each weekend. Raging hormones and sexual energy drives propelled by too much alcohol, weed, and blow frequently erupting into chaos. Two, it's the beginning of many of a young man's and woman's adult life. All this variety makes me happy. It's like Telegraph Ave. in Berkeley, street bums freshly arrived into town from corn fields in Iowa and cow pastures in North Dakota. Hitched a train here, there's not much of a Dinkytown Uprising anymore. It's not the 1960's. That's largely been squelched by the Instagram selfie and the Snapchat filter. Take a selfie with a singing street urchin on your way to the Kitty Cat Klub, it's cheaper than Honey!

One can be cynical and turn your nose up to it all, the absurdity of young adulthood in a "typical college town" in American in 2017, but not me. For me, it's an opportunity for a psychic restart. Repping out my fifth set of squats last night at Los Campeones I seriously joked with my iron brother about the identity of place and how strong I feel it influences my overall state of mind. A move from Uptown to Dinkytown is a move from a bougie hood with overpriced condominiums and shitty trendy 'Merican bars to a place where street bums squatting on the sidewalk brighten my day. It's subtle. I once verbally fought three cops, almost getting arrested last year, in front of the Uptown Apple Store who were sweeping the street clean of a drunk depressed African-American man in front. He was "bad for business." *One less $700 iPhone sold with each of his prayerful swigs of Colt 45. GOD IN HEAVEN IF YOU ARE REAL MAKE IT STOP!* As on Telegraph, in Dinktown the kindness of youth patronizes the lives of the homeless, drunk, and destitute. They might be depressed or schizophrenic. The Dinkytown young might not know the difference, but I do. I know, not that I've been there exactly. I mean I did have a car to live in, but that line is thin and now I see this from a different place. I am not that old, but my iron brother said "you have a young energy."

I always notice her walk in. Sometimes she smiles, and most of the times he grimaces. I smile back and laugh. Next door, I saw the man who dances in cowboy boots and a gothed out skirt at Ground Zero every Saturday night at Bondage-A-Go-Go. I laughed when he said, "I live downtown but come here to feel young." I said so do I, but I live here, and I am young. I live here to play, and to sit in The Bookhouse to gorge on poetry and Heidegger. It's like Moe's Books on Telegraph. It's not that far away where I was Benjamin and she was Mrs. Robinson in the film *The Graduate*:

Mrs. Robinson: Benjamin, I am not trying to seduce you.
Benjamin: I know that, but please, Mrs. Robinson, this is difficult...
Mrs. Robinson: Would you like me to seduce you?
Benjamin: What?
Mrs. Robinson: Is that what you're trying to tell me?
Benjamin: I'm going home now. I apologize for what I said. I hope you can forget it, but I'm going home right now.

Those memories are fresh, but distant here. Mrs. Robinson and I used to dance tango at the Loring Pasta Bar. We used to get pizza at Meza afterwards, but we did not live here in a Dinkytown hovel. The sense of belonging to a place is very strong and is where many of the recent conversations I have had lead. What does it mean to be a self-actualized being? I think, only many years later, it is to know where you come from. It is to know your bloodline and DNA. Not in some kind of fascistic Trumpian way, rather in a way that erases "whiteness" and populates it with diversity. You could be Irish, and be traumatized from a history with the British. You might be a W.A.S.P., traumatized by the pressures of your money and privilege. Religion is here, ethnicity of faith. Peace in the Holy Land, that land of deep passion, good and bad, can be had here over a bowl of hummus and pita at Wally's Falafel and Hummus. I saw while living in Uptown in *Jerusalem: A Cookbook*[21] the following:

Hummus is everybody's favorite food in Jerusalem, and when you talk about something that is so common to everybody but in a place that's so highly divided in many ways, it is already a formula for explosion in many ways. Everybody wants to take ownership of that plate of hummus, both Jews and Arabs, and when this argument starts, there's no end to it...

You could be Jewish-American and not sure what it means to be Orthodox or reformed. You could be Turkish-American and not sure what it means to not know your mother tongue or faith, but feel that you don't quite fit here despite being here. There's only one way to know who you are here, but I can't name it. I cannot put it into language. Words elude me. *It's in the silence of place itself.* It might be to find the trace of your childhood in the ordinary spaces that populate your mundane day. The subtle ways we relate to homogeneity with difference. Asserting our individuality and identity as a rebellion against a bleach that seeks to turn everything the same. This might be the key to creativity and love today for me. I cannot speak for anyone else. I'll just observe and pray, meditate on these small moments. Another smile and another meal. One more day at work, on and on. To what end I don't know, but I am alive and thankful for it. I always notice her walk in, and offer a smile.

---

[21] http://www.nytimes.com/2013/07/31/dining/jerusalem-has-all-the-right-ingredients.html?pagewanted=all

IBM Watson Tone Analyzer Language Analysis:

Emotion

< .5 = not likely present
> .5 = likely present
> .75 = very likely present

Anger		0.13 UNLIKELY
Disgust		0.10 UNLIKELY
Fear		0.13 UNLIKELY
Joy		0.62 LIKELY
Sadness		0.57 LIKELY

Language Style

< .5 = not likely present
> .5 = likely present
> .75 = very likely present

Analytical		0.27 UNLIKELY
Confident		0.00 UNLIKELY
Tentative		0.50 LIKELY

Social Tendencies

< .5 = not likely present
> .5 = likely present
> .75 = very likely present

Openness		0.64 LIKELY
Conscientiousness		0.16 UNLIKELY
Extraversion		0.50 LIKELY
Agreeableness		0.70 LIKELY
Emotional Range		0.37 UNLIKELY

The New Weathers (August 12, 2017)

"The sum of a field's forces [become] what we call very loosely the 'spirit of the place.' To know the spirit of a place is to realize that you are a part of a part and that the whole is made of parts, each of which in a whole. You start with the part you are whole in."

—Gary Snyder

Surrealism these days might be the only way to penetrate it all,

To give it to you as a coherent whole, as a gift, wrapped in a bow,

We know too much, have reduced Her to bits, one's and zero's,

Disembodied, and lost, yet we're here, you're right here, right now,

In this place, embodied, breathing air that I once exhaled, air's old,

The co-rising and interconnectedness of the multiverse, you and I,

This poem came from somewhere, a dream channeled into here,

Into this space, behind a screen, bleeping and pinging, on and on,

This is all a dream, a simulation, I know too much about very little,

Chemistry, atoms in resonance, with you and I here we breath,

In and out, surrealism is dream language and an archive portal,

You can see my memories of facts, and traces of lectures and slides,

That's all gone now, I've got my dreams and my memories, DNA, RNA,

Proteins, and the force fields that guide the way they move and shake,

In reality, in you and I, it's elemental, there are not a hundred elements,

There are four, earth, water, wind, and fire, this is not a delusion, illusion,

To know the parts, and assemble a picture here, in this space take these four,

Combine them in alchemical ratios in your mind, that's all there is, you,

Little I and/or Big I, it does not matter, to know the spirit of place, to meditate,

That is to realize that you are a part of a part and that the whole is made of parts,

Each of which is a whole, you start with the part you are whole in,

For me these four fragments of the hundred, an ancient trace,

No longer a chemist, from now on it's alchemy and alchemy alone,

It's not experiments, it's magic and transmutations, I start where I am, whole,

That is here with this page, and traces of light and dark on a screen and paint,

Paint a picture freely of dreams, and of conscious fragments all bouncing around,

In and out, flowing as words, the wilderness of archive, decolonized mind,

Hive mind, the matrix, wild minds, grids and mappings, I don't see them,

Every trace on this screen I see through to the human on the other side of the desk,

I listen to the voices, this is a real place, a real space and it is here that I live,

Surrealism may be that Jack Kerouac School for Disembodied Poetics,

Gritty and dirty language obsessed with details of pain and suffering,

Only to point up and in, into you and into the sky, only to drop the screen,

To penetrate what is all quite simple, just four elements combined in ratios,

Our weathers, brewing and storming, coherent and fluid this is magic,

Only that alone should you see, here in this place for now, but wait and sit,

Tomorrow will be another day, the friend will call you, and you will drive home,

You will dream, and I will dream, of what only you know, Big I, that master,

The master alchemist in the sky, an illusion of words, but one to pray to just the same.

IBM Watson Tone Analyzer Language Analysis:

Charlottesville, Virginia (August 15, 2017)

There's a necessity to breathe

To smash the chains inside

Through breathes of crystallized patience

To assassinate the fascist inside you

Polemical and angry

Do so now, before the tribulation comes

An immanent black hole

Only selecting those with the right genes

Able to survive in a spacecraft on its way to Mars

The tools are there

To build a new tomorrow

Like Star Trek, universal translator

To understand that we're all the same

DNA, RNA, and protein

Carbon, oxygen, nitrogen, sulfur, phosphorus

Stardust.

IBM Watson Tone Analyzer Language Analysis:

Emotion

< .5 = not likely present
> .5 = likely present
> .75 = very likely present

Anger		0.50 LIKELY
Disgust		0.04 UNLIKELY
Fear		0.04 UNLIKELY
Joy		0.39 UNLIKELY
Sadness		0.09 UNLIKELY

Language Style

< .5 = not likely present
> .5 = likely present
> .75 = very likely present

Analytical		0.16 UNLIKELY
Confident		0.00 UNLIKELY
Tentative		0.18 UNLIKELY

Social Tendencies

< .5 = not likely present
> .5 = likely present
> .75 = very likely present

Openness		0.40 UNLIKELY
Conscientiousness		0.02 UNLIKELY
Extraversion		0.02 UNLIKELY
Agreeableness		0.00 UNLIKELY
Emotional Range		0.28 UNLIKELY

To What Degree? (August 17, 2017)

To what degree do I remain positive

In the face of negative doubt, alone

Cold icy, fans spin beside, airplane

Screams above, rain electric light

Is this techno world like that mud

The mud crusted on my legs, fur

Trail, Grand Portage, hunter-trapper

To some degree I'd rather hunt

Than dance to techno in Dinkytown

From a woman in a robot suit

A millennial's fantasy, I'll sit tonight

This negative memory of the past

Is a blessing and a curse, it's like

Fiction written from a dead man

Only one, but don't mistake it

Most good horror movies start

By digging up graves, anscestors

Indian or Confederate, bad bad

I could blow up Stone Mountain

Like Napoleon shot off the nose

Of the Sphinx to prove a point

It looks a lot like Taliban, old

Dead Stone Buddhas blow up

To make way for a parking deck

Bullshit these negative traces

Are some kind of catalyst, lost.

IBM Watson Tone Analyzer Language Analysis:

Poem Machine (August 16, 2017)

Drove up to Grand Marais, MN and wrote this in the library after talking to a local poet:

How am I feeling?

I am scared for my country with the recent events of this week. I talked to my mother and close friend Alia and wrote a poem with IBM Watson using The Poem Generator.[22] It uses AI algorithms and data about how I am feeling to write a poem to express the feelings and emotions in an appropriate way that is socially acceptable. Poetry hide the raw nature of emotions that come from my insides. I talked to my art therapist and spiritual advisor Maria and she helped me curtail the joy about the fact that I was right we are headed to a second American Civil War. Where does that magma come from when I erupt? Why did I have to run away from the computers at Bite Squad only to fall in love with IBM's AI?

IBM Watson Tone Analyzer Language Analysis of "How am I feeling?":

Pasted the paragraph above into the IBM Watson Poem Generator[23] and got the following output poem:

And far and near the quiet fills
Better than when dust stood between.

Take the far stars for fruit
Asleep, some devil in the mind
The piercing terror cannot see.

...to be continued...

---

[22] https://medium.com/ibm-watson-data-lab/generating-poems-a-way-with-words-and-code-885e85afac4b
[23] http://poem-generator.mybluemix.net/